First edition 2015
Second edition 2018

Yoga Upaniṣad Series *Volume 2*

Yoga Tattwa Upaniṣad

Essence of Yoga

Second edition

Original Sanskrit text with
Transliteration, Translation and Commentary

Swāmī Satyadharma Saraswatī

Sannyāsī Śrimukti (Ruth Perini)

Dedication

To all illumined sages, yogis, rishis and spiritual aspirants

CONTENTS

		Page
Introduction		8
Invocation		15
Verse		
1	Enquiry into the path of yoga	18
2	Viṣṇu, the path and goal	20
3	Brahma's question on yoga	22
4	Web of illusion	24
5, 6	Difficulty of attaining the path	26
7	Indescribable nature of the ultimate consciousness	28
8	The path of liberation	30
9	The big question	31
10	Material evolution	32
11	Paramātmā and jīvatmā	34
12, 13	Causes of bondage	36
14	Removal of the faults	39
15	Path of jñāna and yoga	40
16	Path and goal of jñāna	41
17	Liberation	43
18	About the ultimate knowledge	45
19	Four paths of yoga	46
20	Progression of yoga	48
21, 22	Mantra yoga	49
23	Laya yoga	52
24, 25	Haṭha yoga and rāja yoga	53
26, 27	Inclusion of mudras and bandhas	55
28, 29	Characteristics of yama, niyama and āsana	57
30, 31	Obstacles to yoga	59
32, 33	Sādhana kutir	63
34	Pleasing atmosphere	65
35, 36a	Preparing the seat and beginning the practice	66
36b, 37, 38	Nāḍī śodhana prāṇāyāma	68

39	Continuation of nāḍī śodhana prāṇāyāma	70
40	How to regulate the duration of each breath	72
41, 42	Recommended ratio for nāḍī śodhana	74
43	Number of practice sessions and rounds	76
44, 45	Benefits of nāḍī śodhana	77
46	Leanness of the body; choice of food	79
47, 48, 49	Guidelines during times of practice	81
50, 51a	Kevala kumbhaka—spontaneous breath retention	85
51b, 52, 53a	Three stages of kumbhaka	87
53b, 54, 55	Levitation in kumbhaka	89
56	Importance of secrecy	91
57, 58a	Physical effects of the practice	93
58b, 59, 60a	Power over the earth	95
60b, 61	Power of attraction	97
62	Preservation of semen	98
63	Aum meditation	99
64	First state of perfection	101
65, 66	Second state of perfection	104
67, 68a	Practice of prāṇāyāma	107
68b to 72	Practice of pratyāhāra, sensory control	109
73, 74, 75	Siddhis or powers of yoga	112
76, 77, 78a	Siddhis are obstacles in yoga	115
78b, 79	Assiduous practice	117
80, 81a	Importance of associations and devotion	119
81b, 82, 83a	Awakening of the kuṇḍalinī	122
83b, 84a	Permutation of the five elements	125
84b to 87a	Pṛthvī dhāraṇā	127
87b to 90	Apas dhāraṇā	130
91 to 94a	Agni dhāraṇā	133
94b to 97a	Vāyu dhāraṇā	136

97b to 102a	Ākāśa dhāraṇā	138
102b, 103	Means to attain immortality	143
104 to 106	Dhyāna	145
107 to 108	Samādhi	148
109 to 111	Liberation	151
112 to 115a	Mahābandha	153
115b to 117a	Mahāvedha mudrā	156
117b to 118a	Khecarī mudrā	158
118b, 119a	Jālandhara bandha	160
119b, 120a	Uddiyāna bandha	162
120b, 121a	Yoni or mūla bandha	163
121b to 124a	Viparīta kāraṇi mudrā with mūlabandha	165
124b to 126a	Method of rejuvenation	167
126b, 127	Benefits of vajrolī	170
128, 129a	Amarolī and vajrolī	172
129b to 131a	Kriyās of rāja yoga	174
131b to 134a	Wheel of samsāra	177
134b to 136a	Power of Aum	179
136b to 139a	Meditation on Aum in the heart	182
139b, 140a	Final realization of yoga	184
140b to 142	The stillness of kumbhaka	185
Conclusion		188
Appendices		
1.	Sanskrit Text	189
2.	Guide to Pronunciation	202
3.	Continuous Translation	203
About the Author		219
About the Translator		220

Introduction

Veda is a Sanskrit word meaning 'knowledge'. In the context of the Vedas, it means 'divine knowledge which is *śruti*, 'heard', that is, revealed from within, not taught. These ancient spiritual texts or hymns are grouped into four *saṃhitās* or collections: *Rig Veda, Yajur Veda, Sāma Veda* and *Atharva Veda*. They were revealed to enlightened beings 3,000 to 4,500 years ago or more (the Rig-Veda contains astronomical references describing occurrences in 5,000 to 3,000 BCE), and transmitted orally by the sages from generation to generation within brahmin families.

The four Vedas were considered to be divine revelation, and each word was carefully memorised. This was to ensure accurate transmission, but also because each syllable was considered to have spiritual power, its source being the supreme eternal sound. This was a mammoth task, as there are 20,358 verses in the four Vedas, approximately two thousand printed pages. They were composed in fifteen different metres, which demanded perfect control of the breath. Georg Feuerstein describes them as 'a composite of symbol, metaphor, allegory, myth and story, as well as paradox and riddle' and their composers as 'recipients and revealers of the invisible order of the cosmos [with] inspired insights or illumined visions'. 1

Rig Veda

The Rig Veda is the oldest of the four hymnodies, containing 1,028 hymns or songs in praise of the divine (*rig* or *ric* meaning 'praise'), comprising 10,589 verses. Each hymn is also recognised as a *mantra*, a sacred sound vibration. The illumined seers composed the hymns while established in the highest consciousness, thus able to commune with luminous beings of the higher realms. There are about 250 hymns in praise of *Indra*, the divine force behind the ocean, heavens, thunder, lightning, rain and the light of the sun; 200 of *Agni*, born of the Sun, becoming the god of sacrificial fire, and over 100 of *Soma*, who gives immortality, and who is connected to the Sun, Moon, mountains, rivers and ocean. Others are dedicated to *Varuṇa*, who protects cosmic order; the *Aśvins*, supreme healers; *Uṣās*, goddess of dawn; *Aditi*, goddess of eternity; and *Saraswatī*, goddess of the Vedas and of music and the arts.

Yajur Veda

The hymns of the Yajur-Veda, Veda of Sacrifice, consist of sacrificial formulas or prayers, including those of an internal or spiritual nature. About a third of its 1,975 verses are taken from the Rig Veda. The rest are original and in prose form.

Sāma Veda

The Sāma Veda, Veda of Chants, gives instructions on the chanting of vedic hymns. The majority of its 1,875 verses are from the Rig Veda; only 75 verses are original. Many of the hymns were sung by special priests during sacrificial rites. Some are still sung today.

Atharva Veda

The Atharva Veda, named after the seer Atharvan, whose family were great seers in Vedic times, contains 731 hymns of 5,977 verses, about one fifth of which are from the Rig Veda. Much of the Atharva Veda consists of magical spells and charms for gaining health, love, peace and prosperity, or taking revenge on an enemy. Possibly for this reason, the Atharva Veda was either not accepted by the orthodox priesthood, or given the same standing as the other Vedas.

The vedic people and their culture

The vedic people lived for over 2,500 years mainly along the banks of the Saraswatī River, which was located in Northern India between the modern Rāvi and Yamunā Rivers of habitation included the Ganges River and its tributaries, rivers in Afghanistan (previously called Gandhara), the Himalayas and Mount Kailash in Tibet.

The vedic people had a complex multi-tiered view of the universe, in which humankind, nature and the divine are intertwined and interrelated. They had a deep knowledge of the oceans, mountains, deserts and forests of the physical world, as well as of the subtle worlds of deities and different levels of consciousness. They were also fully engaged in worldly life. People lived in cities or villages or were nomads. Cities were constructed of stone, bricks and metal. They were an agrarian people, yet also had herds of cattle, horses and camels. They built chariots and ships. They were skilled workers in gold, metal, clay, stone, wood, leather and wool, and showed a very high standard in arts, crafts, astrology, medicine, music, dance and poetry.

After the Vedas

The Vedas were the foundation for the later revelations (*śruti*) in the *Brāhmaṇas* (ritual texts), the *Āraṇyakas* (texts on rituals and meditation for forest-dwelling ascetics) and the *Upaniṣads* (esoteric texts). Later still, the Vedas were the basis for numerous works of remembered or traditional knowledge, known as *smṛti,* including the epics: i.e. the *Mahābhārata, Rāmāyaṇa* and *Purāṇas,* and the *Sūtras,* or threads of knowledge, e.g. *Yoga Sūtra.* All these texts contain many concepts and practices which come directly from the four Vedas.

Upaniṣads

The word upaniṣad is comprised of three roots: *upa* or 'near', *ni* or 'attentively', and *ṣad,* 'to sit'. The term actually describes the situation in which these unique texts were transmitted. The students or disciples sat near the realized master and listened attentively, as he expounded his experiences and understanding of the ultimate reality. This teaching was said to destroy the ignorance or illusion of the spiritual aspirant in regard to what is self and non-self, what is real and unreal in relation to the absolute and relative reality.

The Upaniṣads are derived from the Āraṇyakas, because they were chanted in the forest (*āraṇya*) after the aspirant had retired from worldly life. They are considered the last phase of *śruti*, vedic revelation. The Upaniṣads are regarded as *Vedānta*, the end of the Vedas, inferring that Vedānta is the end or completion of all knowledge, as they guide the aspirant to the *ātman* (spiritual self) and thus to *mokṣa* (liberation). Each Upaniṣad reflected the teachings and tradition of a realized master, and was connected with a specific Veda and vedic school. It is estimated that there are over 200 Upanishads, which have been divided into seven groups: Major, *Vedānta*, *Śaiva, Śakta, Vaiṣnava, Sannyāsa* and *Yoga.* The Vedānta and Yoga Upaniṣads are considered the most important.

Yoga Upaniṣads

The twenty one Yoga Upaniṣads give an understanding of the hidden forces in nature and human beings, and describe methods by which these forces can be manipulated and controlled. They emphasise that the inner journey to the one permanent reality, the atman, is the essential one. Journeys to external places, such as holy sites and temples, as well as rituals and ceremonies, are not given importance. Their teachings are concerned with the subtle body, that is, *prāṇa*, *kuṇḍalinī*, *cakras*, *nāḍīs*, as well as descriptions of meditative states, and the tantric and yogic techniques to attain them. Therefore, they are regarded as a significant integration of Vedānta and Tantra, which were previously considered incompatible.

The Yoga Upaniṣads were composed after the *Yoga Sūtras of Patañjali,* and form an important part of the classical yoga literature. However, they contain no references to Patañjali or his Yoga Sūtras. Although the time of compilation of the Yoga Upaniṣads is post-Patañjali, the vidyās, or meditative disciplines ontained within them are pre-Patañjali. The Yoga Upaniṣads were written by vedantic scholars and practitioners in order to show that these vidyās and related practices were not borrowed from Patanjali, but were known and practised from the ancient period.

The following are classified as Yoga Upaniṣads: *Advayataraka, Amṛtanāda, Amṛtabindu, Brahmavidyā, Darśana, Dhyānabindu, Haṃsa, Kṣurika, Mahā Vakyā, Maṇḍalabrāhmana, Nādabindu, Paśupatabrāhmana, Śandilya, Tejobindu, Triśikhibrāhmana, Varāha, Yoga Cudamani, Yogakuṇḍalī, Yogarāja, Yogaśikha* and *Yogatattwa.*

Yogatattwa Upaniṣad

Yogatattwa is a concise and unique text on yoga, as it was known and practised in the early times. The word *tattwa* used here is comprised of two roots: *tat* or 'That' and *twa,* 'essence'. So, the term yogatattwa refers to 'the essence of That', the ultimate reality, which is attainable through yoga. This upaniṣad belongs to the *Kṛṣṇa Yajurveda.* The absence of the author's name from this upaniṣad shows the sentiment of the eminent yogins of this period, who were concerned with spreading the message of Truth, rather than their own personal name and fame.

The teaching conveyed in this upaniṣad begins with a dialogue between Viṣṇu, the supreme godhead, and Brahma, his disciple, who is also the creator of all the manifest worlds. Creation implies the endless process of birth and death, and all the suffering and attachment that arises in-between. Therefore, Brahma inquires from Viṣṇu about the path, which liberates one from the trammels of this cycle. Thus, Viṣṇu enlightens him about the path of yoga, as a means to attain higher states of meditation, and ultimately *moksha*, or liberation.

Yogatattwa Upaniṣad is comprised of 142 verses, which deal with the philosophy, systems and practices of yoga. There are many important topics dealt with here, such as: mantra yoga, laya yoga, haṭha yoga, rāja yoga, the four states of yoga – *ārambhāvasthā*, *ghaṭāvasthā*, *paricayavasthā* and *niṣpattyavasthā.* The text discussses particular practices of yoga, ie: nāḍīśodhan prāṇāyāma, kumbhaka, bandhas, mahāvedha, khecarī mudrā, viparītakaraṇī mudrā, vajrolī mudrā, and amarolī. It further discusses the five *tattwas*, or elements of creation: earth, water, fire, air and ether, and provides detailed instruction on how to meditate upon and realise these elements and their associated powers. The text finally states that, only by the mastery of these practices, is rāja yoga perfected. Dealing with the principle of non-attachment, it explains the practice of Praṇava, meditation on *Aum* in the lotus of the heart. It ends with the discussion of the method of attaining knowledge of the ātman by restraining the senses.

The appendices at the end of the text further provide the reader with a complete version of the Sanskrit text, as well as the pronunciation guide and translation for reference purposes.

It is our hope that by the sincere study of this and other classical texts on yoga, the modern day practitioners and teachers will be able to connect with the roots of yoga, which go back in time to the very dawn of human civilization. By connecting with the antiquity of yoga, a new vision emerges in which one begins to see the vast scope of the practices and the highest aspirations that the yogis of old cherished in their hearts, not only for wellbeing, but for enlightenment and immortality.

References

Saraswati, Swami Satyadharma. *Yoga Chudamani Upanishad* (Yoga Publications Trust, Munger, Bihar, India, 2003)
Aiyar, N.K. *Thirty Minor Upanishads* (Parimal Publications, Delhi, India 2009)
Feuerstein, Georg and Kak, Subhash and Frawley, David. *In Search of the Cradle of Civilization* (Quest Books, Illinois, USA 2001)
1. *ibidem* p.20
Feuerstein, Georg. *The Yoga Tradition* (Hohm Press, Prescott, Arizona USA 2001
Frawley, David. *Gods, Sages and Kings* (Passage Press, Salt Lake City, Utah USA 1991)

योगतत्त्वोपनिषत्
YOGATATTVOPANIṢAT
Essence of Yoga

Invocation

योगैश्वरयं च कैवल्यं जायते यत्प्रसादतः ।

तद्वैष्णवं योगतत्त्वं रामचन्द्रपदं भजे ॥

ॐ सह नाववत्विति शान्तिः ।

yogaiśvaryam ca kaivalyam jāyate yatprasādataḥ

tadvaiṣnavam yogatattvam rāmacandrapadam bhaje
om saha nāvavatviti śāntiḥ

Anvay

prasādataḥ: the blessed one; *jāyate*: is born with; *yoga*: yoga; *ca*: and; *yat*: this; *aiśvaryam*: divine auspiciousness; *kaivalyam*: emancipation; *bhaje*: I worship; *padam*: the feet; *rāmacandra*: of Rāma; *tat:* this; *yogatattvam*: essence of yoga; *vaiṣnavam*: derived from Viṣṇu; *iti*: saying; *avavatu*: may [it] help; *nau*: both of us; *saha*: together; *śāntiḥ*: peace.

Translation of invocation

The blessed one is born in the divine auspiciousness of yoga and emancipation. I worship the feet of Rama, who is the essence of yoga, arisen from Vishnu. Saying: Om, may this teaching benefit both of us together. Peace.

Commentary

Prasad is the gift offered to God, which has been returned, after being received by God, and therefore, carries the divine blessing of God. Rama is that gift, born of Lord Vishnu, into the world of men. He is considered to be a *poorna avatara*, complete form of God, born to man, to live on Earth as a man, for a limited period of time. In this sense, Rama is truly the blessed one, who was born liberated in the highest state of yoga. The author of this Upaniṣad has dedicated the teaching on the essential nature of yoga to the feet of Rāma.

The author's name is not disclosed, perhaps because he is not the original revealer of this knowledge and, therefore, does not consider it to be his own. In ancient times, knowledge such as this, was passed down directly from teacher to disciple over many generations. So, the author may also have heard it from another teacher of his lineage. However, it can be inferred from this invocation that he is a follower of the Vaishnavite tradition, and a devotee of Rama. In the Vedic tradition, each Upaniṣad is linked with a particular Veda. The Yogatattwa Upaniṣad belongs to the Krishna Yajurveda.

Today, yoga is considered to be a science in its own right, but originally, many thousands of years ago, it belonged to the culture of Tantra. The tantric tradition was prominent in the South of the Indian subcontinent, and the vedic tradition in the North. At different times, however, interchanges took between the wise and learned practitioners and teachers of both systems. During these interchanges, vast amounts of spiritual knowledge were passed from one system to another. Afterwards, this knowledge was held, integrated and further disseminated by the tradition of the teachers, who had received it. This would be how the knowledge of yoga came to be held and disseminated by the vedic tradition of Vaiṣnavism.

The invocation ends with the upanishadic *śāntipāṭh*, or invocation of peace, *Om saha nāvavatu*,
which is found above in its abbreviated form. The complete form of this *śāntipāṭh* and its translation are as follows:

Om saha navavatu, saha nau bhunaktu
saha vīryaṃ karavāvahai

tejasvi nāvadhītamastu mā vidviśāvahai

Om śāntiḥ śāntiḥ śāntiḥ

Om ! O Lord, protect us both (teacher and student) together;

Nourish us both together.

May we work together with great energy.

May our study be illumined and clear.

May we have no altercations.

Om ! Peace Peace Peace

Verse 1: Enquiry into the path of Yoga

योगतत्त्वं प्रवक्ष्यामि योगिनां हितकाम्यया ।

यच्छुत्वा च पठितवा च सर्वपापैः प्रमच्यते ।।१।।

yogatattvaṃ pravakṣyāmi yogināṃ hitakāmyayā
yacchutvā ca paṭhitvā ca sarvapāpaiḥ pramucyate (1)

Anvay
pravakṣyāmi: I shall describe; *yogatattvam*: the essence of Yoga; *hitakāmyayā*: with the desire of benefiting; *yoginām*: the yogis; *ca . . . ca*: both . . . and; *śrutvā*: having heard; *paṭhitvā*: having studied; *yat*: this; *pramucyate*: he is freed; *sarvapāpaiḥ*: from all evils.

Translation
I shall describe the essence of Yoga, with the desire of benefiting the yogis. He, who has both heard and studied this, is freed from all evils.

Commentary
Herein begins the discourse on yoga. As a precedent to the teachings, the Rishi, or illumined teacher, clarifies that his aim in disseminating the teaching is not self-oriented. He does not wish to attain name, fame, wealth or glory for himself, but to benefit the yogis of all lineages and times. We can assume that in his time, as well as now, the true teacher and path of yoga were very hard to come by. There may have been persons, who claimed to know, but whose knowledge was imperfect or incomplete. Therefore, in declaring his desire to benefit others by this teaching, the Rishi shows his true nature and integrity.

The complete yoga can only be revealed to a worthy student by the yogin, who has fully mastered and traversed the path. The realized teacher, the worthy student, and the true teachings are the three requisites of the yoga path described here. These three form a triangle, which represents the conditions for the transmission of true yoga. Yogatattwa is the essence or truth of yoga, which is eternal, and remains one and the same for all time. Those yoga students, who have heard this teaching and then have studied it, and put it into practice, will free themselves of all negative propensities. With the removal of darkness, only the light remains. It should be observed, however, that the mere hearing of, or reading about, the path will not suffice. In order to attain the fullness of yoga, the student must put it into practice.

Verse 2: Viṣṇu, the path and goal

विष्णुर्नाम महायोगी महाभूतो महातपाः ।
तत्त्वमार्गे यथा दीपो दृश्यते पुरुषोत्तमः ।।२।।
viṣṇurnāma mahāyogī mahābhūto mahātapāḥ
tattvamārge yathā dīpo dṛśyate puruṣottamaḥ (2)

Anvay

mahāyogī: the great yogin; *mahābhūtaḥ*: the great being; *mahātapāḥ*: the great ascetic;
viṣṇuḥ: Viṣṇu; *nāma*: by name; *puruṣottamaḥ*: the Supreme Spirit; *dṛśyate*: is seen; *yathā*: like; *dīpah*: a light; *mārge*: on the way; *tattva*: to the essence.

Translation

The great yogin, the great being, the great ascetic is Viṣṇu by name. He, the Supreme Spirit, is seen like a light on the way to the essence.

Commentary

Viṣṇu is the name of God, revered in the Vaiṣṇav tradition, as the *Puruśottama*, or highest, supreme spirit. The name Viṣṇu does not refer to any one personage as such, but represents the universal consciousness, which pervades all beings, sentient and insentient, manifest and unmanifest, and also exists beyond them in the highest truth, which is untouched by space, time and object. Hence, Viṣṇu, the unborn universal consciousness, is the essence of all beings and forms of existence, and at the same time, ever retains its own unlimited and pure expansiveness, which is untouched by any quality or limitation of name and form, birth and death.

This verse also refers to Viṣṇu as: the great yogin, the great ascetic, and the great being, for these three are all aspirants and seekers of the universal truth, and as such, they each embody it to some degree on this earthly plane. The yogin seeks to attain Viṣṇu, the supreme consciousness, through the practices of yoga and meditation, the ascetic through a life of penance, hardship and endurance, and the great person, through meritorious and exemplary acts. In this sense, He, the supreme being, is the universal light, which is seen by those, who travel the path of self-realization or enlightenment. This light is what guides the seeker on his chosen path towards the true essence of himself and of all existence. So, Viṣṇu, the eternal, ever-expanding consciousness, is both the path and the goal for the seekers, and therefore, the knowledge contained in this upaniṣad is dedicated to Him.

Verse 3: Brahma's question on yoga

तमाराध्य जगन्नाथं प्रणिपत्य पितामः।
पप्रच्छ योगतत्त्वं मे ब्रूहि चाष्टाङ्गसंयुतम् ।।३।।
tamārādhya jagannāthaṃ praṇipatya pitāmaḥ
papraccha yogatattvaṃ me brūhi cāṣṭāṅgasaṃyutam

Anvay
pitāmaḥ: paternal grandfather (Brahma); *ārādhya*: having served; *praṇipatya*: having prostrated; *jagannātham*: protector of the world (Viṣṇu); *papraccha*; asked; *tam*: him; *brūhi*: describe; *me*: to me; *yogatattvam*: the essence of yoga; *ca*: and; *samyutam*: the joining together; *aṣṭāṅga*: of its eight components.

Translation
The paternal grandfather (Brahma), having served and prostrated to the protector of the world (Viṣṇu), asked him: 'Describe to me the essence of yoga and the joining together of its eight components'.

Commentary
Although Viṣṇu is the supreme consciousness, the origin of all existence, both manifest and unmanifest, he brings about the creation through Brahma, who is his evolute, or his first mind-born son. Brahma is therefore considered to be the lord of all manifest creation, and hence the paternal grandfather of all beings in creation.

Brahma is the creative force of Viṣṇu. He is the creator of all the manifest worlds in existence. Brahma is symbolized as a deity with four heads, enabling him to gaze into every direction. The creator must be all-seeing and all-knowing in order to manifest the creation. Brahma arises from the navel of Viṣṇu, seated upon a lotus flower, which represents his pure origin. He is the creative power of the universal, supreme consciousness.

In this verse, Brahma first serves and prostrates before his father, Viṣṇu, the ultimate source and Lord of the world. Through service and prostration, one is able to open oneself to and connect oneself with the higher forces, and receive their guidance and wisdom. Then, having offered his respects, Brahma asks his father, Viṣṇu, to explain to him the essence of yoga, the union between the individual and supreme consciousness.

This question regarding the essence of yoga is a very deep subject, which must be known to Brahma, as he is the progenitor of all the individual beings in creation. It is only with the evolution of manifest beings that unity with the unmanifest consciousness becomes relevant. Brahma also asks for a description of the eight limbs of yoga, which are the means for living beings to achieve this unity. The eight limbs include: (1) *yama*, codes of external conduct, (2) *niyama*, codes of internal conduct, (3) *āsana*, posture, (4) *prāṇāyāma*, breath control, (5) *pratyāhāra*, sensory withdrawal, (6) *dhāraṇā*, one pointed concentration, (7) *dhyāna*, unbroken continuity of meditation, and (8) *samādhi*, transcendental meditation.

Verse 4: Web of illusion

तमुवाच हृषीकेशो वक्ष्यामि शृणु तत्त्वत: ।
सर्वे जीवा: सुखैर्दु:खैर्मायाजालेन वेष्टिता: ।।४।।

tamuvāca hṛṣīkeśo vakṣyāmi śṛṇu tattvataḥ
sarve jīvāḥ sukhairduḥkhairmāyājālena veṣṭitāḥ (4)

Anvay
hṛṣīkeśaḥ: another name for Viṣṇu, controller of the senses; *uvāca*: said; *tam*: to him; *śṛṇu*: listen; *vakṣyāmi*: I will explain; *tattvataḥ*: thoroughly; *jīvāḥ*: living beings; *veṣṭitāḥ*: are trapped; *sarve*: always; *jālena*: by the web; *māyā*: of illusion; *sukhaiḥ-duḥkhaiḥ*: in happiness [and] sorrow.

Translation
Hṛṣīkeśaḥ said to him: 'Listen, I will explain thoroughly: living beings are always trapped by the web of illusion in happiness and sorrow.

Commentary
Hṛṣīkeśaḥ is another name for Viṣṇu. He is also known as the 'controller of the senses', because this is the requisite quality of one, who remains ever merged in the the absolute consciousness. This question on yoga, being very mysterious, requires a thorough explanation in order to understand it. Such an explanation can only be given by one, who has complete mastery of the subject. Similarly, it can only be understood by one who is totally receptive to the master and the teaching. Therefore, this verse also shows the time-honoured relationship between the master and the disciple, which has always existed from the first moment of creation.

So, Guru instructs the disciple to listen carefully. He first explains that the path of yoga is necessary for living beings, because they are enmeshed in the web of illusion. All embodied beings are deluded by the idea of individuality, which arises from birth. Due to their identity with the body, they forget their true nature, which is consciousness, and begin to experience the external world as the reality. The individual being, who is identified with the body and the world, is always susceptible to the play of opposites: pain and pleasure, loss and gain, happiness and sorrow, which are the outcome of every interaction in life. This play of opposites gives rise to anxiety, fear and confusion, which cause suffering, and further obscure the individual's understanding of himself and of life.

Verses 5 and 6: Difficulty of attaining the path

तेषां मुक्तिकरं मार्गं मायाजालनिकृन्तनम् ।

जन्ममृत्युजराव्याधिनाशनं मृत्युतारकम् ।।५।।

नानामार्गैस्तु दुष्प्रापं कैवल्यं परमं पदम् ।

पतिताः शास्त्रजालेषु प्रज्ञया तेन मोहिताः ।।६।।

teṣāṃ muktikaraṃ mārgaṃ māyājālanikṛntanam
janmamṛtyujarāvyādhināśanaṃ mṛtyutārakam (5)
nānāmārgaistu duṣprāpaṃ kaivalyaṃ paramaṃ padam
patitāḥ śāstrajāleṣu prajñayā tena mohitāḥ (6)

Anvay
tu: but; *kaivalya*: emancipation; *paramam*: supreme; *padam*: abode; *duṣprāpam*: difficult to reach; *nānāmārgaiḥ*: by different ways; *teṣām*: of these (ways); *mārgam*: the way; *mukti-karam*: leads to liberation; *nikṛntanam*: destroying; *māyā-jāla*: the web of illusion; *nāśanam*: eliminating; *janma*: birth; *mṛtyu*: death; *jarā*: old age; *vyādhi*: disease; *tārakam*: delivering from; *mṛtyu*: death; *patitāḥ*: those fallen; *śāstra-jāleṣu*: among the webs of teachings; *mohitāḥ*: are deluded; *tena*: by that; *prajñayā*: knowledge.

Translation
But, *kaivalya*, the supreme abode, is difficult to reach by different ways. Of these, the way (to kaivalya) is the one which leads to liberation, destroying the web of illusion, eliminating birth, death, old age [and] disease, [and] delivering [the aspirant] from death. Those fallen among the web of teachings are deluded by that knowledge.

Man's mistaken identity with the body and the world becomes the cause of his infinite suffering. In order to correct this erroneous conception, it is necessary to realize the true nature of oneself and the world, which is the unlimited, ever expansive consciousness. This realization is known as *kaivalya*, merging into the supreme abode of consciousness. Although this infinite consciousness pervades all beings and existence, it is very difficult to attain. There are thousands of paths and systems of higher knowledge in the world, and teachers abound who would elucidate them.

However, kaivalya, the experience of the supreme, all pervading consciousness, is almost impossible to reach by these. The way that leads to kaivalya is the path of liberation. This is a practical and experiential path, which destroys the web of illusion, wrong identification and suffering. The seeker of truth, who follows this path, is able to eliminate the causes of suffering: birth, disease and old age, and is delivered from death. However, those who are enmeshed in the different systems of teachings become deluded by that knowledge, and are unable to attain the ultimate experience of kaivalya.

Verse 7: Indescribable nature of the ultimate consciousness

अनिर्वाच्यं पदं वक्तुं न शक्यं तैः सुरैरपि ।

स्वात्मप्रकाशरूपं तत्किं शास्त्रेण प्रकाश्यते ।।७।।

anirvācyaṃ padaṃ vaktuṃ na śakyaṃ taiḥ surairapi
svātmaprakāśarūpaṃ tatkiṃ śāstreṇa prakāśyate

Anvay

na: not; *śakyam*: possible; *api*: even; *taiḥ suraiḥ*: for the gods; *vaktum*: to describe; *padam*: a place; *anirvācyam*: indescribable; *tatkim*: how; *rūpam*: a form; *Prakaasha*: illuminated; *Svaatma*: by its own Self; *prakāśyate*: can be illuminated; *śāstreṇa*: by teachings.

Translation

[It is] not possible even for the gods to describe a place [which is] indescribable. How can a form [already] illuminated by its own Self be illuminated by [any] teachings?

Commentary

Within the infinite strata of creation there are thousands of *lokas*, or planes of existence, which are instinctive, human and divine. Some levels, such as our world, have myriad material forms, both sentient and insentient, which exist for specified periods of time. There are also higher planes, which are beyond form, beyond duality. Even the gods are unable to describe such a plane or dimension of being, which exists beyond form, because there is no object to describe and no subject to describe it. The pathway to liberation leads to this dimension, which is beyond form, beyond subject and object, beyond duality. The absolute consciousness is self-arisen and is illumined by its own self. Hence, Viṣṇu, who is that very form of luminous consciousness, asks, how can the self-illumined consciousness be illuminated by any form of teachings?

Verse 8: The path of liberation

निष्कलं निर्मलं शान्तं सार्वातीतं निरामयं ।
तदेव जीवरूपेण पुण्यपापफलैर्वृतम् ॥८॥
niṣkalaṃ nirmalaṃ śāntaṃ sarvātītaṃ nirāmayam
tadeva jīvarūpeṇa punyapāpaphalairvṛtam (8)

Anvay

eva: just; *tat*: that; *niṣkalam*: undivided; *nirmalam*: unsullied; *śāntam*: calm; *atītam*: gone beyond; *sarva*: all; *nirāmayam*: welfare; *vṛtam*: chosen; *jīvarūpeṇa*: by a living form; *phalaiḥ*: by the fruits; *punya*: good deeds; *pāpa*: evil deeds.

Translation

Just that, [which is] undivided, unsullied, calm and has gone beyond all welfare, is chosen by a living form with the fruits of good and evil deeds.

Commentary

A person, living in the world, is chosen to tread the path of liberation by the fruits of his or her good and evil deeds. If the accumulated karmas, or actions, of a person are unripened or unsuitable, he or she will not be chosen to walk this path. The path to kaivalya leads one inward to the experience of oneness, where the consciousness remains undivided. This experience goes beyond all forms or ideals of happiness and wellbeing. It just is... that.

Verse 9: The big question

परमात्मपदं नित्यं तात्कथं जोवतां गतम् ।
सर्वभावपदातोतं ज्ञानरूपं निरञ्जनम् ।।९।।
paramātmapadaṃ nityaṃ tatkathaṃ jīvatāṃ gatam
sarvabhāvapadātītaṃ jñānarūpaṃ nirañjanam (9)

Anvay
katham: how; *tat*: that; *padam*: seat; *paramātma*: Supreme Soul; *nityam*: eternal; *atītam*: beyond; *pada*: the state; *sarva*: all; *bhāva*: existing things; *rūpam*: the form; *jñāna*: of wisdom; *nirañjanam*: pure; *gatam*: did pass to; *jīvatām*: of the living.

Translation
How did that, which is the seat of the supreme soul, eternal [and] beyond the state of all existing things, [and is] pure [and] has the form of wisdom, pass to [the state] of the living?

Commentary
This verse poses the age-old question... If that consciousness is the seat of the supreme soul, that exists in the unmanifest, beyond the state of all manifest things, is eternal, all knowing, perfect, and pure, how then did it pass into the state of the living, manifest existence, which has none of these qualities?

Verse 10: Material evolution

वारिवात्स्फुरितं तासमिस्तात्राहंकृतिरुत्थिता ।
पञ्चात्मकमभूत्पिण्डं धातुबद्धं गुणात्मकम् ।।१०।।
vārivatsphuritaṃ tasmistatrāhaṃkṛtirutthitā
pañcātmakamabhūtpiṇḍaṃ dhātubaddhaṃ guṇātmakam (10)

Anvay

tatra: there; *ahaṃkṛtiḥ*: *ahamkara* (individual ego); *utthitā*: brought forth; *tasmin*: in this; *vat*: like; *vāri*: water; *sphuritam*: suddenly arising; *piṇḍam*: a body; *ātmakama*: consisting of; *pañca*: five; *bhūta*: elements; *guṇa*: *guṇas* (three qualities of nature); *baddham*: bound by; *dhātu*: seven layers of the body: flesh, blood, digestive juice, fat, bone, marrow, semen.

Translation

There, the *ahaṃkāra* brought forth in this, like [a bubble] suddenly arising in the water, a body consisting of the five elements, of the three *guṇas*, and bound by the seven *dhātus*.

Commentary

That supreme consciousness, being the source of all manifest existence, yet ever unmanifest in itself, requires a path and evolutes in order to become manifest. In the evolution of different beings, the supreme or universal consciousness, which exists in the state of eternal oneness, must first become individuated, so that the One may become many. Therefore, the first evolute of consciousness is *ahaṃkāra*, the individual ego, or sense of personal identity. What was One, now sees itself as an individual consciousness, which is separate from the whole.

The verse describes the emerging of ego, like a bubble suddenly arising in water. In this analogy, the bubble, which has been chosen to represent the arising of ego, appears to be an entity, but in reality it is a phantasm, empty, having no substance at all. The bubble arises suddenly from water in the same way that the ego arises from the unmanifest consciousness. The adjective 'suddenly' is used here to indicate the transition from stillness to movement, from the unmanifest to the manifest. When there is no creation, there is no movement. The first evolute, therefore, seems to appear suddenly out of the depths of the unmanifest.

With the arising of the first evolute, or ego identity, the path of evolution is set into motion. Ahaṃkāra, the identity of the individual conscious field, next requires a body in which to live and interact on the worldly plane. So from ego, the five elements of: (i) space, (ii) air, (iii) fire, (iv) water and (v) earth, combine and permutate to form a material body. These five elements are influenced by the three *guṇas*, or qualities of nature, which are: (i) *tamas*, stability; (ii) *rajas,* motion; and (iii) *sattwa*, balance. The different possible combinations of the guṇas and elements is infinite, and thus the multitude of beings comes into existence.

This transition from the formless state of existence into individual forms is bound into place with the further permutation of the seven *dhātus*, which are the fundamental tissue layers of the body responsible for its formation, support and survival. These seven dhātus are the evolutes of the five elements. All earthly beings are influenced by the dhātus, which give substance and structure to the tissues, organs and systems of the body. The seven dhātus are as follows: (i) *rasa*, lymph or fluid; (ii) *rakta*, blood; (iii) *mansa*, muscle; (iv) *meda*, fat and hormones; (v) *asthi*, bone and connective tissue; (vi) *majja*, bone marrow and nerves; (vii) *śukra*, reproductive fluid.

Verse 11: Paramātma and jīvātma

सुखदु:खै: समायुक्तं जोवभावनया कुरु ।
तेन जोवाभिधा प्रोक्ता विशुद्धै: परमात्मनि ।।११।।
sukhaduḥkhaiḥ samāyuktaṃ jīvabhāvanayā kuru
tena jīvābhidhā proktā viśuddhaiḥ paramātmani (11)

Anvay
kuru: perceive; *samāyuktam*: joined with; *sukha-duḥkhaiḥ*: happiness and sorrow; *viśuddhaiḥ*: purified; *bhāvanayā*: through the production of; *tena*: thus; *abhidhā*: term; *jīva*: embodied consciousness; *proktā*: revealed; *paramātmani*: in the supreme self.

Translation
Perceive that which is joined with happiness and sorrow, which has been purified, is through the production of *jīva.* Thus the term *jīva* is revealed in the supreme self.

Commentary
Try to understand that the consciousness, which remains ever pure, unlimited and free in itself, has for some indeterminable reason, manifested an ego, or individual identity, and a body in which to dwell on earth for a limited period of time. By virtue of the ego in the body, the consciousness is able to connect and interact with the beings in the world around it. Thus the idea of duality develops, because the ego experiences itself as separate from other beings. So, there is always I and other, which is the basis for all action. In this way, the one field of all-knowing consciousness, which exists behind the ego and the body, is joined with pleasure and pain, and experiences happiness and sorrow with each interaction of the body in the world.

When the consciousness, which is the real self, remains in the unembodied state, it is called *paramātma*, the highest or supreme self. But when that consciousness becomes embodied and lives in the world, it is called *jīvātma*, the living self. The paramātma is eternal, unbound and free, but the jīvātma becomes bound while living in the body. The living consciousness becomes identified with the body, and is thus limited by this perception of itself. As attachment develops for the material persona and the things of the world, the consciousness becomes bound by them. This is how the jīvātma, which is bound by the condition of living in the body, relates to the paramātma, which is unbound and, therefore, ever free. In this way the embodied self is revealed by the unembodied self.

Verses 12 and 13: Causes of bondage

कामक्रोधभयं चापि मोहलोभमदो रज: ।
जन्म मृत्युश्च कर्पन्यं शोकस्तन्द्रा क्षुधातृषा ।।१२।।
तृष्णा लज्जा भयं दु:ख: विषादो हर्ष एव च ।
एभिर्दोषैर्विनिर्मुक्त: स जोव: केवलो मत: ।।१३।।
kāmakrodhabhayaṃ cāpi mohalobhamado rajaḥ
janma mṛtyuśca kārpaṇyaṃ śokastandrā kṣudhātṛṣā (12)
tṛṣṇā lajjā bhayaṃ duḥkhaṃ viṣādo harṣa eva ca
ebhirdoṣairvinirmuktaḥ sa jīvaḥ kevalo mataḥ (13)

Anvay

sa jīvaḥ: that embodied soul; *mataḥ*: is thought; *kevalaḥ*: complete; *vinirmuktaḥ*: freed from; *ebhiḥ*: these; *doṣaiḥ*: faults; *kāma*: lust; *krodha*: anger; *bhayam*: fear; *ca*: and; *api*: also; *moha*: delusion; *lobha*: greed; *mada*: pride; *raja*: passion; *janma*: birth; *mṛtyu*: death; *kārpaṇyam*: miserliness; *śokaḥ*: grief; *tandrā*: laziness; *kṣudhā*: hunger; *tṛṣā*: thirst; *tṛṣṇā*: craving; *lajjā*: shame; *bhayam*: fright; *duḥkham*: sorrow; *viṣādaḥ*: despair; *ca*: and; *harṣaḥ*: exultation; *eva*: as well.

Translation

That embodied soul is thought [to be] complete [when] freed from these faults: desire, anger, fear and also delusion, greed, pride, lust, birth and death, miserliness, grief, laziness, hunger, thirst, craving, shame, fear, sorrow, despair and exultation as well.

Commentary

Although the *jīvātma*, embodied consciousness, is of the same stuff as the *paramātma*, the unembodied consciousness, it is considered to be impure, limited and bound, due to its proximity and identification with the body and the world. Whereas the supreme consciousness, having no worldly contact or influence, is pure and free. The jīva can only be freed from bondage, and thus return to its homogeneous state, where it is complete in itself, when all the associations, which arise from contact with the material world, have been rooted out. These associations are regarded as *doṣa*, or faults, due to their limiting effect on the consciousness. They are the experiences of the self in the world of duality, the most fundamental being *janma*, birth, and *mṛtyu*, death, which are the unavoidable outcomes of association with the body that is born, lives for a period of time, and then dies.

In-between birth and death, while the body is living in the world, the other doṣa, or defects, arise. The six basic faults of the jiva, or living consciousness, which arise due to worldly contact, are mentioned in this verse: (1) *kāma*, desire, attraction, (2) *krodha*, anger, aversion, (3) *bhaya*, fear, (4) *lobha*, greed, (5) *moha*, delusion, and (6) *mada*, pride. All spiritual texts and traditions speak about the importance of removing these six faults; otherwise, the aspirant will be unable to progress on the spiritual path. These faults are also described as the great enemies of the yogi, or the great fires, which destroy the outcome of all yogic practice and penance.

The first of these six enemies is desire, the initial cause of birth itself and of all the positive tendencies. The second is aversion, the opposite to desire and the cause of all the negative propensities. Where there is attraction or liking, there will also be aversion or disliking. Together desire and aversion represent the first two steps of the ego into the world of duality, and they act as the catalyst for all the other faults, which arise in the course of life. The primary outcome of desire and aversion is the third enemy, fear. The jīva fears that it will not get what it likes, and again fears that it will get what it dislikes. So, due to desire and aversion, fear is ever-present in the life of the jīva, regardless of its position or situation in the world. Ever-fearful, the jīva suffers anxiety and stress, and knows no peace within himself or in the world around him.

From desire also springs the fourth enemy, greed. When something is very attractive and desirable, one wants to have more and more of it. The stronger the desire, the greater the greed. Under the influence of greed, one can never have enough of the desired object. The fifth enemy is delusion, or erroneous perception. The jīva becomes attached to the notion that the body and the world around it are permanent and real, and forgets its true nature, which is consciousness. This misidentification is the root of all troubles, because material beings and objects are impermanent; only consciousness is permanent. The identification with all that is impermanent causes suffering. The sixth enemy is pride whereby the ego feels satisfaction with itself and its achievements, which are not founded in the reality of consciousness, but in the illusive existence of the world.

From these six enemies of the self, a further host of faults arises. Desire and attachment give rise to craving, a continual longing, yearning or hankering for the pleasurable objects or persons, which can never be satisfied. From craving arises miserliness, because the desired object, once obtained, should never leave one's sight or be lost. Birth leads to perpetual hunger and thirst; while death brings sorrow and grief. Success brings pride and exultation, while failure brings despair and remorse. Failure to live and behave in accordance with truth leads to shame. Unwillingness to work for one's welfare or salvation leads to laziness and lack of motivation. Each of these faults creates obstruction and obscures the light of consciousness. Only by the removal of these faults will the true nature, which is pure consciousness, complete in itself, be revealed.

Verse 14: Removal of the faults

तस्माद्दोषविनाशार्थमुपाय: कथयामि ते ।
योगहीनं कथं ज्ञानं मोक्षदं भवति ध्रुवम् ।।१४।।
tasmāddoṣavināśārthamupāyaṃ kathayāmi te
yogahīnaṃ kathaṃ jñānaṃ mokṣadaṃ bhavati dhruvam (14)

Anvay
tasmāt: thus; *kathayāmi*: I shall tell; *te*: you; *upāyam*: means; *artham*: purpose; *vināśa*: destruction; *doṣa*: faults; *katham*: how; *jñānam*: higher knowledge, wisdom; *hīnam*: which omits; *yoga*: practices leading to union with the supreme consciousness); *bhavati*: can be; *dhruvam*: sure; *dam*: to give; *mokṣa*: liberation.

Translation
Thus I shall tell you the means and purpose for the destruction of these faults. How can that knowledge, which omits yoga, be sure to give liberation?

Commentary
Now, the means and the purpose will be discovered for the destruction and removal of the human faults, which obscure the true nature of consciousness. These faults perpetuate a false notion of ego-body-self existing in a constantly changing world, through the perception of the senses and their objects. The purpose for the destruction of these faults is the attainment of *jñāna*, direct knowledge of the reality of consciousness. The means or method to remove these faults and attain jñāna is yoga, the practical science of liberation, which unites the jīvātma with the paramātma, the limited or bound consciousness with the supreme or complete consciousness. The verse then asks, how can knowledge, the purpose alone, be sure to give liberation in the absence of yoga, which provides the practical means or path of attainment?

Verse 15: Path of jñāna and yoga

योगो हि ज्ञानहीनस्तु न क्षमो मोक्षकर्मणि ।
तस्माज्ज्ञानं च योगं च मुमुक्षुर्दृढमभ्यसेत् ।।१५।।
yogo hi jñānahīnastu na kṣamo mokṣakarmaṇi
tasmājjñānaṃ ca yogaṃ ca mumukṣurdṛḍhamyaset (15)

Anvay
tu: but; *hi*: surely; *yoga*: practices leading to union with the supreme consciousness; *hīnaḥ*: without; *jñāna*: higher knowledge, wisdom; *na*: not; *kṣamaḥ*: favourable for; *karmaṇi*: the effect; *mokṣa*: of liberation; *tasmāt*: thus; *mumukṣuḥ*: the seeker of liberation; *dṛḍhamyaset*: must be established in; *ca . . . ca*: both . . . and; *jñāna*: knowledge; *yoga*: *yoga*.

Translation
But surely yoga without *jñāna* [is] not favourable for the effect of liberation. Thus the seeker of liberation must be established in both jñāna and yoga.

Commentary
Here, the other side of the question is presented. Just as jñāna in the absence of yoga will not be a sure path to attain liberation; similarly, the practice of yoga in the absence of jñāna will not lead to liberation. In order to progress on any given path, the objective or goal must be known. Jñāna is the knowledge of paramātma, the supreme consciousness, which is necessary to progress on the path of yoga. In the absence of this knowledge, the practice of yoga will have no ultimate goal or outcome. Interestingly, this describes the path of yoga, which is prevalent today: yoga for fitness, yoga for relaxation, but not yoga for the liberation of consciousness. Only this path will lead to a definite and sure outcome.

Verse 16: Path and goal of jñāna

अज्ञानादेव संसारो ज्ञानादेव विमुच्यते ।
ज्ञानस्वरूपमेवादौ ज्ञानं ज्ञेयैकसाधनम् ।।१६।।
ajñānādeva saṃsāro jñānādeva vimucyate
jñānasvarūpamevādau jñānaṃ jñeyaikasādhanam (16)

Anvay
saṃsāraḥ: cycle of birth, death and rebirth; *eva*: only; *ajñānāt*: from ignorance; *vimucyate*: is released; *jñānāt*: through knowledge; *ādau*: at the beginning; *jñāna*: knowledge; *eva*: indeed; *svarūpam*: the very embodiment; *jñāna*: of knowledge; *eka*: the only; *sādhanam*: means; *jñānam*: for knowledge; *jñeya*: to be understood.

Translation
The cycle of saṃsāra (birth, death and rebirth) [occurs] only due to *ajñāna* (ignorance) [and] is released through *jñāna* (knowledge). In the beginning, *jñāna* [was] indeed the very embodiment of knowledge [and was] the only means for *jñāna* to be understood.

Commentary
All beings in creation are subject to the cycle of saṃsāra, which is the process of birth and death. Generally, life is considered as a celebration, but in yoga and spiritual life, it is also seen as a condition undergone by the soul, which is fraught with pain and suffering. From the time of conception, the being undergoes much discomfort in the tight confines of the womb. After the pain of birth and emerging suddenlyinto the light of the external world, it experiences the difficulties of growth and subjugation by parents and teachers. In all the stages of life, it is susceptible to disease, which is inborn and also transmitted from the environment. Finally old age ensues with its onslaught of pains and limitations, followed by the fear and transition of death and ultimately rebirth.

The embodied being undergoes this cycle of saṃsāra due to *ajñāna*, ignorance of its true nature, which is ever-expanding consciousness. Once born in the body, the soul enters a state of forgetfulness, wherein it identifies with the material world around it, and loses sight of its real nature. There is no escape from this cycle for the living being, except through the path of jñāna, which leads to reunion with the inner knowledge of consciousness. When the being is able to reunite with the light of its own consciousness, the ignorance and suffering caused by its misidentification with the world is removed.

The verse states that from the very beginning of all existence, jñāna was the self-born inner knowledge of the consciousness. Thus, jñāna is the only means, by which this knowledge of the self can be understood. In the light of the sun, all darkness disappears. Similarly, in the light of knowledge, all ignorance and suffering are removed. The cycle of saṃsāra can no longer bind the being, who is illumined with self-knowledge. Such a being lives in the world, but not of it, and therefore does not undergo the suffering of life in the same way as one, who is identified with the world and ignorant of the self.

Verse 17: Liberation

ज्ञातं येन निजं रूपं कैवल्यं परमं पदम् ।
निष्कलं निर्मलं साक्षात्सच्चिदानन्दरूपकम् ।।१७।।
jñātaṃ yena nijaṃ rūpaṃ kaivalyaṃ paramaṃ padam
niṣkalaṃ nirmalaṃ sākṣātsaccidānandarūpakam (17)

Anvay
yena: by it; *paramam*: supreme; *padam*: seat; *jñātam*: is known; *sākṣāt*: directly; *nijam*: indwelling; *nirmalam*: unsullied; *niṣkalam*: undivided; *rūpam*: form; *kaivalyam*: of emancipation; *rūpakam*: consisting of the form of; *sat-cit-ānanda*: the supreme reality as existence-consciousness-bliss.

Translation
By it (jñāna), the supreme seat is known directly as the indwelling, pure, undivided form of *kaivalya*, consisting of the form of *sat-cit-ānanda.*

Commentary
The seat of the supreme consciousness, which dwells within all beings, can only be known by jñāna, direct inner knowledge of the self. This knowledge cannot be known by the mind or senses; it cannot be seen or heard or received in any way from any outside source. The experience of this pure, unlimited and undivided form of consciousness is called *kaivalya*, or liberation. The word kaivalya comes from the root *kevala*, meaning 'one only'. This seat of supreme consciousness is the superconscious state, where all duality, which relates with name, form object and idea, is transcended.

In kaivalya, only the one universal consciousness remains. This is the highest state of samādhi, also known as *mokṣa* or *nirvāṇa*. This supreme, liberated consciousness has three qualities: (1) *sat*, truth absolute, ultimate existence, (2) *cit*, consciousness, totality of knowing, and (3) *ānanda*, bliss. In this state only these three qualities of consciousness are known. There is only truth, only knowing, only bliss. So this experience is described by the yogins, who have attained it, as *satcitānanda*.

Verse 18: About the ultimate knowledge

उत्पत्तिस्थितिसंहारस्फूर्तिज्ञानविवीर्जतम् ।
एतज्ज्ञानमिति परोक्तमथ योगं ब्रवीमि ते ।।१८।।
utpattisthitisaṃhārasphūrtijñānavivīrjatam
etajjñānamiti proktamatha yogaṃ bravīmi te (18)

Anvay
vivīrjatam: beyond; *jñāna*: knowledge; *sphūrti*: appearance; *utpatti*: creation; *sthiti*: maintenance; *saṃhāra*: dissolution; *iti*: thus; *etat*: this; *proktam*: was said; *jñāna*: knowledge; *atha*: now; *bravīmi*: I shall describe; *yogam*: yoga; *te*: to you.

Translation
[It is] beyond the knowledge and appearance [of] creation, maintenance and dissolution. Thus, this was said about *jñāna*. Now I shall describe yoga to you.

Commentary
The experience of the supreme, undivided, unlimited consciousness, is beyond the knowledge and perception of worldly appearances. It is beyond the universal cycle of existence. The universe comes into being with all of its galaxies, planets and stars, through the process of creation. It is then sustained for millions of ages through the process of maintenance, and ultimately it goes through the process of dissolution, in order to be born anew once again. Jñāna is the ultimate knowledge of the supreme, unborn consciousness which exists beyond and behind all of the manifest existence and its cycles. This much has been said about jñāna.

Now Viṣṇu, the transmitter of this teaching, will describe yoga to Brahma.

Verse 19: Four paths of yoga

योगो हि बहुधा ब्रह्मन्भिद्यते व्यवहारत: ।
मन्त्रयोगो लयश्चैव हठो ऽसौ राजयोगत: ।।१९।।
yogo hi bahudhā brahmanbhidyate vyavahārataḥ
mantrayogo layaścaiva haṭho 'sau rājayogataḥ (19)

Anvay
brahman: O Brahman; *yoga*: yoga; *bhidyate*: is divided; *bahudhā*: in many parts; *vyavahārataḥ*: namely; *mantrayogaḥ*: mantra yoga; *layaḥ*: laya yoga; *ca*: and; *haṭhaḥ*: hatha yoga; *eva*: as well; *asau*: that; *rājayogataḥ*: in accordance with rāja yoga

Translation
O Brahman, yoga is divided into many parts, namely: mantra yoga, laya yoga and haṭha yoga, as well; that is in accordance with rāja yoga.

Commentary
In this verse Brahma, the seeker of knowledge, is addressed as Brahman by Viṣṇu, the Lord and the teacher of this upaniṣad. In the ancient vedic tradition the Brahmans were considered to be of superior intellect. Therefore, they were considered to be most worthy, receptive and capable of understanding this pinnacle of knowledge. Having explained jnana, the highest knowledge and attainment of human endeavour, the teacher begins to speak about yoga, the path to jñāna.

The word yoga means 'union', and pertains to the union of the individual with the supreme consciousness. Yoga is not the philosophy or the meaning of this union, but the practical means by which to achieve it. The verse says that the science of yoga is divided into many parts. There are many paths to reach the one supreme consciousness, because there are many types of individual beings, who walk them. Different people have different natures and qualities; therefore different paths of yoga are required to facilitate their journey.

Viṣṇu speaks here of the four main yogas, which were known and practised in his time. (1) *Mantra yoga* is the liberation of mind through the principle of sound. The word mantra comes from the term *mananāt trayati*, or liberation of the mind. (2) *Laya yoga* is the yoga of dissolution, whereby the individual consciousness is dissolved into the supreme consciousness. (3) *Haṭha yoga* is the yoga of balancing the sun and moon, the vital and mental energies, and thereby awakening the kundalini force. (4) These three yogas were to be known and practised in accordance with *rāja yoga,* the yoga of meditation. Rāja yoga was known as the kingly yoga, for only the most powerful practitioners were able to face the mind by the mind.

Verse 20: Progression of yoga

आरम्भश्च घटश्चैव तथा परिचय: स्मृत: ।
निष्पत्तिश्चेत्यवस्था च सर्वत्र परिकीर्तिता ।।२०।।
ārambhaśca ghaṭaścaiva tathā paricayaḥ smṛtaḥ
niṣpattiścetyavasthā ca sarvatra parikīrtitā (20)

Anvay
tathā: therefore; *ārambhaḥ*: beginning stage; *ghaṭaḥ*: second stage; *paricayaḥ*: third stage; *ca*: and; *eva*: indeed; *niṣpattiḥ*: fourth and final stage; *smṛtaḥ*: prescribed; *ca*: and; *iti*: thus; *avasthā*: state; *sarvatra*: always; *parikīrtitā*: proclaimed.

Translation
Therefore, the beginning stage, the second, third and indeed the fourth and final stage [are] prescribed, and thus [this] state is always proclaimed.

Commentary
In the previous verse, the four yogas that were widely known at the time when this upaniṣad was taught, are mentioned. In this verse the application of these yogas is further indicated. First, mantra yoga should be practised, followed by laya yoga, then haṭha yoga and finally rāja yoga. This was the recognised progression of yoga to be observed by a sincere aspirant. In this context, however, it should be considered that yoga is not a static system, but an evolutionary science, which has been adapted to the developing and changing needs of humanity in every age. Therefore, the progression of yogas utilized by practitioners in the past may not be suitable or applicable for the level of seekers today.

Verses 21 and 22: Mantra yoga

एतेषाः लक्षणं ब्रह्मन्वक्ष्ये शृणु समासतः ।
मातृकादियुतं मन्त्रं द्वादशाब्दं तु यो जपेत् ।।२१।।
क्रमेण लभते ज्ञानमणिमादिगुणान्वितम् ।
अल्पबुद्धिरिमं योगं सेवते साधकाधमः ।।२२।।
eteṣāṃ lakṣaṇaṃ brahmanvakṣye śṛṇu samāsataḥ
mātṛkādiyutaṃ mantraṃ dvādaśabdaṃ tu yo japet (21)
krameṇa labhate jñānamaṇimādiguṇānvitam
alpabuddhirimaṃ yogaṃ sevate sādhakādhamaḥ (22)

Anvay

brahman: O Brahman; *śṛṇu*: listen; *vakṣye*: I shall describe; *samāsataḥ*: concisely; *lakṣaṇam*: characteristic; *eteṣām*: of these; *yaḥ*: whoever; *japet*: should repeat; *mantram*: sacred sounds; *dvādaśabdam*: for twelve years; *mātṛkāt*: *mātṛkās,* Sanskrit letters; *iyutam*: together with; *krameṇa*: gradually; *labhate*: obtains; *jñānam*: *jñāna*; *ādi*: beginning with; *aṇimā*: *aṇiman* one of eight siddhis, the power of making the body subtle; *anvitam*: possessing; *guṇa*: attributes of nature; *adhamaḥ*: most inferior; *sādhaka*: *sādhaka,* spiritual aspirant; *alpabuddhiḥ*: of little intelligence; *sevate*: practises; *imam*: this; *yogam*: *yoga.*

Translation

O Brahman, listen! I shall describe concisely the characteristic[s] of these [yogas]. Whoever should repeat the mantra for twelve years together with the syllables, gradually obtains jñāna, beginning with the power of making the body subtle and light, and the knowledge of guṇa, the qualities of nature. The most inferior aspirant of low intelligence practises this yoga.

Commentary

Here begins a brief but comprehensive explanation of the attributes of these four yogas, starting in this verse with mantra yoga. The teacher asks the student to listen carefully in order to avoid any confusion or misunderstanding, as these yogas are very distinct. Mantras are not ordinary words; they are specific and special sounds of power, which were to be received directly from a mantra master. The repetition of mantra is known as japa, and is one of the major practices of meditation in yoga. The teacher says that the aspirant, who repeats the mantra with awareness of the *matrikas*, the sounds of each letter comprising the mantra, for twelve years together, will gradually attain jñāna, self-knowledge.

On the path of mantra meditation, the sādhaka encounters the eight *siddhis*, yogic powers or perfections, beginning with *anima*, the ability to make the body very light and subtle. Lightness of the body is necessary in order to enter deeper states of meditation. When a person is very worldly, the body is correspondingly heavy and gross. By the continued repetition of mantra, the vibratory field of the body becomes purified and harmonized. This leads to a feeling of lightness and increased perception, which allows the practitioner to enter into deeper states of meditation.

In the course of mantra meditation, with the increase of lightness and perception, the sadhaka becomes aware of the *guṇas*, or qualities of nature, and their influence in every aspect of life. All beings at all times are influenced by three qualities of nature: (1) *tamas*: stability or inertia, (2) *rajas*: activity or dynamism, and (3) *sattwa*: balance or purity. In order to progress in meditation the guṇas or qualities must be understood. When tamas and rajas are predominant, meditation will not be successful. Only when sattwa predominates is meditation fruitful. Therefore, knowledge of the gunas and the ability to regulate them is an important requisite, and it is an outcome of mantra yoga.

In yoga, all practitioners are not considered to be equal. According to the predominant guṇa, a person's nature may be more or less developed and ready for yoga. The verse says that mantra yoga is suitable even for the most inferior sādhaka, who is of tamasic nature and possesses little intelligence and motivation. By the practice of mantra yoga, such a sādhaka will be able to attain jñāna.

Verse 23: Laya yoga

लययोगश्चित्तलय: कोटिश: परिकीर्तित: ।
गच्छन्तिष्ठन्स्वपन्भुञ्जन्ध्यायेन्निष्कलमीश्वरम् ।।२३।।
layayogaścittalayaḥ koṭiśaḥ parikīrtitaḥ
gacchanstiṣṭhansvapanbhuñjandhyāyenniṣkalamīśvaram (23)

Anvay
layayogaḥ: *laya yoga*; *layaḥ*: dissolution; *citta*: *citta*, individual consciousness; *parikīrtitaḥ*: is described; *koṭiśaḥ*: in innumerable ways; *dhyāyet*: one should meditate on; *niṣkalam*: absolute; *īśvaram*: Lord; *gacchan*: moving; *tiṣṭhan*: resting; *svapan*: sleeping; *bhuñjan*: eating.

Translation
Laya Yoga, dissolution of individual consciousness, is described in innumerable ways. One should meditate on the absolute Lord [while] moving, resting, sleeping [or] eating.

Commentary
Although laya yoga is not well known today, it was an important yoga in previous times. The word *laya* means 'dissolution'. In this yoga the individual, limited mind is dissolved into the universal, unlimited consciousness. The rishi says there are innumerable ways in which laya yoga may be practised. One of the ways, which he mentions here, is meditation on the absolute Lord during the course of one's daily activities. The absolute Lord is another way of saying the supreme or universal consciousness. The Lord, whether he be represented in human form, divine form, or God himself, is always immersed in the highest consciousness. So to meditate on the Lord is to connect oneself with the supreme consciousness. The mind of the sadhaka, who is aware of the Lord, even while moving through life, resting, eating and sleeping, will gradually drop worldly identifications and dissolve into the universal consciousness.

Verses 24 and 25: Haṭha yoga and rāja yoga

स एव लययोगः स्याद्धठयोगमतः शृणु ।
यमश्च नियमशचैव आसनं प्राणसंयमः ।।२४।।
प्रत्याहारो धारणा च ध्यानं भ्रूमध्यं हरिम् ।
समाधिः समतावस्था साष्टाङ्गो योग उच्यते ।।२५।।
sa eva layayogaḥ syāddhaṭhayogamataḥ śṛṇu
yamaśca niyamaścaiva āsanaṃ prāṇasaṃyamaḥ (24)
pratyāhāro dhāraṇā ca dhyānaṃ bhrūmadhyaṃ harim
samādhiḥ samatāvasthā sāṣṭāṅgo yoga ucyate (25)

Anvay
sa: this; *syāt*: must be; *layayogaḥ*: *laya yoga*; *śṛṇu*: listen to; *haṭhayogamataḥ*: that which is *haṭha yoga*; *yoga*: yoga; *ucyate*: is said; *sāṣṭāṅgaḥ*: with eight limbs; *yamaḥ*: ethical behavior; *ca*: and; *niyamaḥ*: inner discipline; *ca eva*: and indeed; *āsanam*: steady physical posture; *prāṇasaṃyamaḥ*: *prāṇāyāma*, breathing techniques which expand the life force; *pratyāhāraḥ*: withdrawal of the senses; *dhāraṇā*: concentration; *dhyānam*: meditation; *harim*: Hari, Viṣṇu; *bhrūmadhyam*: eyebrow centre; *samādhiḥ*: pure awareness; *samata-avasthā*: state of equilibrium.

Translation
This must be laya yoga. Listen to that which is haṭha yoga. Yoga is said [to have] eight limbs: yama and niyama, and indeed āsana, prāṇāyāma, pratyāhāra, dhāraṇā, and dhyāna (meditation on Viṣṇu at the eyebrow centre), [leading to] samādhi, the state of equilibrium.

Commentary
Having explained laya yoga briefly, the teacher continues to speak on haṭha yoga. This discussion will continue throughout the rest of the upaniṣad. After asking his disciple to listen to the teachings on haṭha yoga, he proceeds to

enumerate the eight limbs, which are regarded as the components of raja yoga: (1) *yama*, the external disciplinary codes of yoga; (2) *niyama*, the internal disciplinary codes of yoga; (3) *āsana*, physical postures; (4) *prāṇāyāma*, breathing practices; (5) *pratyāhāra*, sensory withdrawal; (6) *dhāraṇā*, one-pointed attention; (7) *dhyāna*, unbroken flow of meditation; and (8) *samādhi*, transcendental meditation. We may infer that the verse combines the teaching of haṭha yoga and rāja yoga into one system, which is then termed as 'yoga'. Perhaps the first four limbs, which are known as *bahiraṅga*, or the external limbs of yoga, were to be considered as haṭha yoga, and the last four limbs, which are known as *antaraṅga*, the inner limbs of yoga, as rāja yoga.

It is also of interest to note that in defining dhyāna, the seventh limb, the teacher speaks of meditation on Viṣṇu at *bhrūmadhya*, the eyebrow centre. Viṣṇu is the guru or master of the knowledge conveyed in this upaniṣad. He is further the luminary, which represents God, or the universal consciousness, as described in verse 2. Bhrūmadhya, the trigger point for ajña cakra, is located at the eyebrow centre. Ajña cakra is also known as the guru cakra, where the disciple may be guided in deep states of meditation by the inner voice of the guru. Finally the verse describes samādhi, the highest limb of yoga, as the state of equilibrium, in the sense that it is totally beyond all duality and multiplicity.

Verses 26 and 27: Inclusion of mudrās and bandhas

महामुद्रा महाबन्धः महावेधश्च खेचरी ।
जालंधरोद्दियाणश्च मूलबन्धस्तथैव च ।।२६।।
दीर्घप्रणवसंधानं सिद्धान्तश्रवणं परम् ।
वज्रोली च अमरोली च सहजोली त्रिधामता ।।२७।।
mahāmudro mahābandho mahāvedhaśca khecarī
jālaṃdharoddiyāṇaśca mūlabandhastathaiva ca (26)
dīrghapraṇavasaṃdhānaṃ siddhāntaśravaṇaṃ param
vajrolī cāmarolī ca mahajolī tridhāmatā (27)

Anvay
mahāmudraḥ: combination of mūlabandha and śambhavi mudra; *mahābandhaḥ*: combination of mūlabandha, uddiyāna bandha and jālandhara bandha; *ca*: and; *mahāvedhaḥ*: great piercing mudra; *khecarī*: tongue lock; *jālandhara*: chin lock; *uddiyānaḥ*: abdominal lock; *tathā-eva*: likewise; *mūlabandhaḥ*: perineal lock; *saṃdhānam*: meditation; *praṇava*: mantra Aum; *dīrgha*: for a long time; *śravanam*: listening to; *param*: highest; *siddhānta*: truth; *tridhāmatā*: triad; *vajrolī*: urinary lock; *amarolī*: drinking of one's own urine; *sahajoī*: smearing the body with a special paste of ashes after performing vajrolī.

Translation
[This yoga also includes practices of mudrā and bandha:] mahā mudrā, mahā bandha and mahā vedha, khecarī mudrā, jālandhara bandha, uddiyāna bandha, and likewise mūla bandha, [as well as] chanting the mantra *Aum* for a long time, listening to the highest truth, and the triad of vajrolī, amarolī and sahajolī.

Commentary
Having discussed the eight limbs of yoga in the previous verse, the teacher adds that the mudrās and bandhas are also

important aspects of yoga, although they are not enumerated in the eight limbs, which include only āsana and prāṇāyāma, as the third and fourth limbs. He mentions the major mudrās and bandhas, which are important components of haṭha, kuṇḍalinī and kriyā yogas. The mudras, which he includes here are: mahā mudrā, mahābheda mudrā, khecarī mudrā, along with the triad vajrolī mudrā, sahajolī mudrā and amarolī, which is not actually a mudra, but involves the drinking of one's own urine, as a purification practice. The bandhas are: jālandhara bandha, uddiyāna bandha, mūla bandha, and mahā bandha.

Along with the mudrās and bandhas, the rishi mentions meditation on the *praṇava*, or mantra *Aum*, which is recommended here to be practised for long durations of time. This form of mantra meditation has been highly respected from ancient times as a means to reconnect the sādhaka with the supreme consciousness, as the sound *Aum* is the first emanation or vibration of creation. He further adds that listening to the highest truth, as in attending satsang or spiritual discussions, is an important aspect of yoga, because this will explain the direction and the ultimate outcome of the yoga practices.

Verses 28 and 29: Characteristics of yama, niyama and āsana

एतेषां लक्षणं ब्रह्मन्प्रत्येकं शृणु तत्त्वत: ।
लध्वाहारो यमेष्वेको मुख्यो भवति नेतर: ।।२८।।
अहिंसा नियमेष्वेका मुख्या वै चतुरानन ।
सिद्धं पद्मं तथा सिंहं भद्रं चेति चतुष्टयम् ।।२९।।
eteṣāṃ lakṣaṇaṃ brahmanpratyekaṃ śṛṇu tattvataḥ
ladhvāhāro yameṣveko mukhyo bhavati netaraḥ (28)
ahiṃsā niyameṣvekā mukhyā vai caturānana
siddhaṃ padmaṃ tathā siṃhaṃ bhadraṃ ceti catuṣṭayam (29

Anvay
brahman: O Brahman; *śṛṇu*: listen; *tattvataḥ*: attentively; *pratyekam*: each; *lakṣaṇam*: characteristic; *eteṣām*: of these; *caturānana*: O Four-faced one (Brahma); *yameṣu*: amongst the *yamas*; *laghu-āhāraḥ*: light eating; *bhavati*: is; *ekaḥ*: single; *mukhyaḥ*: chief; *netaraḥ*: factor; *niyameṣu*: amongst the *niyamas*; *ahiṃsā*: non-violence; *vai*: definitely; *ekā mukhyā*: most important; *tathā*: likewise; *catuṣṭayam*: four; *iti*: namely; *siddham*: siddhāsana, accomplished pose; *padmam*: padmāsana, lotus pose; *siṃham*: siṃhāsana, lion pose; *ca*: and; *bhadram*: bhadrāsana, gracious pose.

Translation
O Brahman, listen attentively to each characteristic of these [limbs]. Amongst the *yamas*, light eating is the single chief factor. Amongst the *niyamas*, non-violence
is definitely the most important, O four-faced one. Likewise, [there are] four [main postures]: *siddhāsana*, *padmāsana*, *siṃhāsana* and *bhadrāsana*.

Commentary
Here Brahma, as the brāhmin disciple, is exhorted to listen carefully as the main attributes of the eight limbs of yoga are

given. He is later referred to as the 'Four-Faced one', a common appellation, as Brahma has four heads. This discussion begins with the first two limbs, and here it must be remembered that the yama and niyama of haṭha yoga are different to those delineated in rāja yoga. The yama, which is given precedence here, is eating lightly. Heavy food is tamasic, and therefore, counter-productive to the practice of yoga. It makes the body and mind heavy, and predisposes one to digestive ailments of all kinds. Light food, taken in moderation, is sattwic, and so conducive to yoga. A light diet requires less time and energy to digest, allowing more time and energy for the practice. As a simple guideline, one should allow two hours to elapse before practising after a light meal and four hours after a heavy meal.

Of the niyamas, non-violence is said here to be the most important. Non-violence is the first tenet in all spiritual traditions. Violence, whether in thought, word or deed, disturbs the mind of the practitioner, as well as the environment all around, and makes it very difficult to progress in yoga. Violence enhances the tamasic and rajasic gunas, while peace and harmony promote sattwa. Yoga practices balance the system and increase sattwa. Therefore, it is necessary for the serious practitioner to refrain from all types of violent behaviour, and to establish the practice in a peaceful and harmonious environment.

In regard to āsana, the third limb of yoga, the four main postures are given: (1) *siddhāsana*, adept posture, (2) *padmāsana*, lotus posture, (3) *siṃhāsana*, lion posture, and (4) *bhadrāsana*, pleasing posture. These are the four main meditative postures, and are mentioned in preference to all the other āsanas, because haṭha yoga leads to rāja yoga. The ability to sit comfortably in a meditative posture with the spine erect for long durations of time is a main requisite of yoga. Each of these postures hold the body in an ideal position for the unfolding of higher states of consciousness.

Verses 30 and 31: Obstacles to yoga

प्रथमाभ्यासकाले तु विघ्नः स्युश्चतुराननन् ।
आलस्य कत्थनं धूर्तगोष्टी मन्त्रादिसाधनम् ।।३०।।
धातुस्त्रीलौल्यकादीनि मृगतृष्णामायानिवै ।
ज्ञात्वा सुधीस्त्यजेत्सर्वान्विघ्नान्पुण्यप्रभावतः ।।३१।।
prathamābhyāsakāle tu vighnāḥ syuścaturānan
ālasya katthanaṃ dhūrtagoṣṭī mantrādisādhanam (30)
dhātustrīlaulyakādīni mṛgatṛṣṇāmāyāni vai
jñātvā sudhīstyajetsarvānvighnānpuṇyaprabhāvataḥ (31)

Anvay
tu: but; *caturānan*: O Four-faced One; *kāle*: time; *prathama*: early; *abhyāsa*: practice; *syuhu*: following; *vighnāḥ*: obstacles; *ālasya*: laziness; *katthanam*: boasting; *goṣṭī*: company; *dhūrta*: fraudulent; *sādhanam*: *sādhana*, spiritual practice; *ādi*: beginning with; *mantra*: sacred sounds; *laulakya:* desire for; *dhātu*: metals; *strī*: women; *ādīni*: etcetera; *vai*: indeed; *māyāni*: illusions; *mṛga*: craving; *tṛṣṇā*: greed; *jñātvā*: knowing; *sudhīḥ*: wise man; *tyajet*: should relinquish; *sarvān vighnān*: all obstacles; *puṇya*: virtuous; *prabhāvataḥ*: powers.

Translation
But, O Four-faced One, the following obstacles [arise]: time of early practice, laziness, boasting, the company of fraudulent people, beginning sādhana with mantra, desire for metals and women etc, [and] indeed illusions of craving and greed. Knowing [this], a wise man should relinquish all obstacles through [his] virtuous powers.

Commentary
The limbs of yoga are clearly set out, O Brahma (Four-faced one), but the path is beset with numerous obstacles, which make it difficult for practitioners to progress. The first difficulty, which many aspirants face, is to get up early in the

morning and perform the yoga practice at the time of *brahmamuhūrta*, between four and six am. This is a special period in the day, when God is said to walk the earth, so it is the optimal time for yoga practice. The atmosphere is peaceful and sublime, so regular practice at this time will yield good results. However, arising early in the morning on a regular basis is difficult, unless one goes to bed early in the evening. Again, it is not possible to retire early, unless the evening meal is taken early. In this way, it becomes evident that lifestyle changes and commitment are necessary in order to avoid this first obstruction, which is the early time of practice.

The second obstruction is laziness, which nearly every practitioner falls prey to at some point in the sādhana. Laziness arises from the influence of tamas. In the morning one wishes to remain in the bed, rather than get up early and start the practice. In the evening one prefers to turn on the television or have a drink, rather than retire early for the practice. Any activity that is easy and effortless would be preferred to the practice, when one is feeling lazy. If the practitioner gives in to laziness, it will become chronic, and the practice will come to a halt. When the practice stops due to laziness, it is very difficult to begin again. So, laziness is a very powerful obstruction. The practitioner must be aware and take great care to handle it correctly.

The third obstruction is boasting. The desire to boast arises when one has some success or achievement in sādhana. Pride is one of the six major deterrents to spiritual life, and boasting is an expression of this attribute. Boasting depletes one's spiritual merit and grace, and leads to disappointment and downfall. There are some things, which a person should never talk about. One of these is the experiences, which arise during sādhana. A practitioner may have wonderful and illumining visions during the course of sādhana, but these are just indications of what is to come. They do not denote any particular achievement or power in themselves, and usually disappear in time, never to return again. The practitioner, who feels proud and boasts of these experiences, will feel doubly disappointed and lost, when they no longer manifest during the sādhana. This may even cause one to leave the sādhana.

The fourth obstruction to sādhana is bad associations. The company one keeps is very important, because it has a powerful influence on the mind. The main objective of yoga sadhana is to discover and awaken the mind. Bad company dissipates and clouds the mind, and leads one away from sadhana. The practitioner must constantly be on guard against negative influences. One hour of bad company is detrimental to sādhana and may take hours and even days to undo. In order to maintain a continuity in sādhana, the mind should be kept in a calm and optimistic state. The practitioner should avoid the company of friends, relatives and associates, who have a discouraging influence and keep the mind stirred up. Ultimately a choice must be made between those associations and the sādhana.

The fifth obstruction is beginning sādhana with mantra. Yoga sādhana is very scientific and specific. Mantra is a method of meditation. Yoga practice should begin with āsana, followed by prāṇāyāma, mudra and bandha, then relaxation and finally meditation. By adhering to this sequence, the body, energy and mind are prepared, balanced and focussed for the practice of meditation. If one ignores this sequence, or performs the practices out of sequence, the result may not be favourable. The mind is very subtle and the awareness must be attuned to it gradually and systematically. The external awareness of the world is very different to the internal awareness of the mind. The practitioner, who begins the sādhana with mantra meditation, will often be lost in hypnotic states, without attaining inner awareness and clarity.

The sixth obstruction to sādhana is the desire for wealth and women. This is the age-old warning that is found in all spiritual traditions. In order to be regular in sādhana, one's spiritual resolve must take priority over all material attainments and enjoyments. The desire for wealth takes one in the opposite direction to sādhana, and uses up a lot of time and energy, which would otherwise be dedicated to attaining one's spiritual goals. Similarly, the desire for sexual interaction is equally or even more disturbing and consuming. Sexual stimulation draws the energy down to the lower centres and makes it very difficult to concentrate or meditate on anything other than the object of its fulfillment. These two desires should be satisfied, or one should feel that their fulfillment is not necessary for one's happiness, before taking up a regular sadhana,. Otherwise, there will be continual conflict between the desires and the sādhana, and the strongest will always win out.

The seventh obstruction is craving and greed. Craving means that once a desire is fulfilled, one wants to experience it again and again. Continual hankering for the things of the world disturbs the mind and draws it away from the practice. Greed arises when one takes more than one needs and more than one's share. Both craving and greed result in strong material attachment, which holds one in bondage to the objects and associations of the world. The ultimate purpose of yoga and meditation is *mokṣa*, liberation from worldly bondage and attachment.

So, knowing this, the wise person renounces these seven obstructions by the power of his or her virtuous nature and actions. It is not easy to avoid these seven obstacles to the yogic path, while living in the world. Many have tried, but few have succeeded. That is why the sincere sādhaka is considered to be of upright and noble character, having cultivated self-control and ethical behaviour in every situation and circumstance.

Verses 32 and 33: Sādhana kutir

प्राणायामं ततः कुर्यात्पद्मासनगतः स्वयम् ।
सुशोभनं मठं कुर्यात्सूक्ष्मद्वारं तु निर्व्रणम् ।।३२।।
सुस्थुं लिप्तं गोमयेन सुधया वा प्रयत्नतः ।
मत्कुनैर्मशकैर्लूतैर्वर्जितं च प्रयत्नतः ।।३३।।
prāṇāyāmaṃ tataḥ kuryātpadmāsanagataḥ svayam
suśobhanaṃ maṭhaṃ kuryātsūkṣmadvāraṃ tu nirvraṇam (32)
susṭhuṃ liptaṃ gomayena sudhayā vā prayatnataḥ
matkunairmaśakairlūtairvarjitaṃ ca prayatnataḥ (33)

Anvay
tu: now; *kuryāt*: he should make; *suśobhanam*: beautiful; *matham*: monastic hut; *sūkṣma*: narrow; *dvāram*: doorway; *nirvranam*: without cracks; *susṭhum*: well; *liptam*: smeared; *gomayena*: with cowdung; *vā*: or; *sudhayā*: with mortar; *ca*: and; *prayatnataḥ*: carefully; *varjitam*: cleared of; *matkunaiḥ*: bugs; *maśakaiḥ*: mosquitoes; *lūtaiḥ*: spiders; *tataḥ*: then; *gataḥ*: having gone into; *padmāsana*: *padmāsana*, lotus pose; *kuryāt*: he should practise; *prāṇāyāma*: *prāṇāyāma*, breathing practices; *svayam*: by himself.

Translation
Now he should make a beautiful monastic hut with a narrow doorway, without cracks, well-smeared with cow-dung or mortar, and carefully cleared of bugs, mosquitoes [and] spiders. Then, having gone into padmāsana, he should practise prāṇāyāma by himself.

Commentary
Here the place of sādhana is described. The idea that a special place should be constructed expressly for the practice of yoga shows the level of seriousness and dedication to the practice, which the yogis of old had. After diligently rooting

out the seven obstructions within oneself, which in itself is a gigantic task for any person living in the world, the aspirant searches for an appropriate place to retire to for the practice of yoga. This place should be free of smoke, pollution, noise, proximity of violent or ignoble persons, and distractions of all kinds.

In such a place, the dedicated practitioner should construct a beautiful *kutir,* or cottage, to be used exclusively for the practice of yoga. The sādhana kutir should be small and proportional, and pleasing to the aesthetics. It should be constructed from natural materials with a narrow door and no windows. Windows are for seeing out, but during yogic practice, one should be intent upon seeing within. The narrow door is to discourage the entry of any other persons or creatures, apart from the sādhaka. The floor and walls of the kutir should be free of cracks and smeared regularly with the paste of cow-dung or clay. Cow-dung is considered to be a pure and natural substance. It has antiseptic properties and keeps bacteria, mould and insects away. Any cracks in the walls should be filled in to prevent the entry of insects and small creatures.

The kutir should be carefully cleaned each day to remove dust, insects, mosquitoes and spiders, whose movement would disturb the sādhana. Then sitting down, by oneself, in padmāsana, the lotus posture, the sādhaka should begin the practice of prāṇāyāma. The word *swayam*, by oneself, alone, is indicative of an important requisite for higher sādhana. In the beginning the yoga aspirant learns and practises yoga in a group with several others, but ultimately, the practice must be continued alone, without the proximity of other persons to engage one's attention.

Verse 34: Pleasing atmosphere

दिने दिने च संमृष्टं समार्जन्या विशेसतः ।
वासितं च सुगन्धेन धूपितं गुग्गुलादिभिः ।।३४।।
dine dine ca saṃmṛṣṭaṃ samārjanyā viśeṣataḥ
vāsitaṃ ca sugandhena dhūpitaṃ guggulādibhiḥ (34)

Anvay
Dine Dine: every day; *viśeṣataḥ*: specially; *saṃmṛṣṭam*: swept; *samārjanyā*: with a broom; *vāsitam*: imbued with; *sugandhena*: pleasant fragrances; *ca*: and; *dhūpitam*: perfumed; *guggulādibhiḥ*: sweet-smelling gum.

Translation
Every day [the sādhana kutir should be] specially swept with a broom, imbued with pleasant fragrances and perfumed with sweet-smelling gum.

Commentary
A pleasing atmosphere is important for regularity and success in the practice of yoga. The mind should be tranquil, positive and happy in the environment, where the practices are undertaken. It is said that cleanliness is godliness. So, each day the sādhana kutir should be dusted and swept clean with a special broom, which is made from sweet smelling grasses. The room is then permeated with natural fragrances, such as incense or sweet smelling herbs and gums.

Verses 35 and 36(a): Preparing the seat and beginning the practice

नात्युच्छ्रितं नातिनीचं चैलाजिनकुशोत्तरम् ।
तत्रोपविश्य मेधावी पद्मासनसमन्वित: ।।३५।।
ऋजुकाय: प्राञ्जलिश्च प्रणमेदिष्टदेवताम ।३६।
nātyucchritaṃ nātinīcaṃ cailājinakuśottaram
tatropaviśya medhāvī padmāsanasamanvitaḥ (35)
ṛjukāyaḥ prāñjaliśca praṇamediṣṭadevatām (36a)

Anvay
upaviśya: having sat down; *tatra*: there; *samanvitaḥ*: assumed; *padmāsana*: lotus pose; *uttaram*: on a pile; *caila*: cloth; *ajina*: deerskin; *kuśa*: *kuśa* grass; *na-ati-ucchritam*: not very high; *na-ati-nīcam*: not very low; *medhāvī*: wise man; *kāyaḥ*: body; *ṛju*: upright; *ca*: and; *prāñjaliḥ*: his clasped hands respectfully outstretched; *praṇamet*: should bow down; *iṣṭa-devatām*: *iṣṭa devata*, personal deity;

Translation
Having sat down there [and] assumed padmāsana on a cushion of cloth, deerskin [and] *kuśa* grass, not very high [and] not very low, the wise man, his body upright and his clasped hands respectfully outstretched, should bow down to his personal deity.

Commentary
After preparing the space for sādhana, the practitioner then prepares the seat. The traditional seat for the practice of yoga was very specific and also scientific. The seat should be of medium height, not too high and not too low. This means there should be a feeling of connection and balance with the earth. This connection may be lost, when the seat is too elevated. At the same time, the seat is to be somewhat elevated for comfort and also to avoid the disturbance of any insect or creature, which may crawl in from outside.

The seat was generally comprised of three layers: a pile of kuśa grass on the bottom, covered by a deer skin, and finally a clean cotton cloth placed on the top. Kuśa grass creates a cushion for the buttocks and hips, and is also an excellent energy conductor. The deer skin has auspicious properties for yoga, as the deer is known to be gentle, non-violent, alert and fleet. The cotton cloth placed on the top is again for comfort and also absorption.

Having prepared the seat, the practitioner sits upon it in the position of padmāsana with the body upright. Before beginning the yoga practice, the wise person respectfully clasps his hands together, stretches his arms forward, and bows down to his *iṣṭa devata,* personal deity. Here the iṣṭa devata may be a mental concept or a picture or image of one's personal deity, which may be placed strategically to one side of the sādhana kutir. The verse speaks of the wise man, who would first offer this respect to the personal form of God. Before beginning any undertaking, it is auspicious to remember one's goal, and in yoga, the ultimate goal is union with the divine.

Verses 36(b), 37 and 38: Nāḍī śodhana prāṇāyāma

ततो दक्षिणहस्तस्य अङ्गुष्ठेनैव पिङ्गलाम् ।।३६।।
निरुध्य पूरयेद्वायुमिडया तु शनैः शनैः ।
यथाशक्त्यविरोधेन ततः कुर्याच्च कुम्भकम ।।३७।।
पुनस्त्यजेत्पिङ्गलया शनैरेव न वेगतः ।
पुनः पिङ्गलयापूर्य पूरयेदुदरं शनैः ।।३८।।
tato dakṣiṇahastasya aṅguṣṭhenaiva piṅgalām (36b)
nirudhya pūrayedvāyumiḍayā tu śanaiḥ śanaiḥ
yathāśaktyavirodhena tataḥ kuryācca kumbhakam (37)
punastyajetpiṅgalayā śanaireva na vegataḥ
punaḥ piṅgalayāpūrya pūrayedudaraṃ śanaiḥ (38)

Anvay

tataḥ: then; *nirudhya*: having closed; *piṅgalām*: right nostril; *aṅguṣṭhena*: thumb; *dakṣiṇa-hastasya*: of his right hand; *vāyum pūrayet*: he should inhale; *śanaiḥ śanaiḥ*: very slowly; *iḍayā*: through the left nostril; *ca*: and; *tataḥ*: then; *avirodhena*: without pausing; *kuryāt*: he should perform; *kumbhakam*: breath retention; *yathāśakti*: for as long as he can; *tyajet*: he should exhale; *punaḥ*: again; *piṅgalayā*: through the right nostril; *eva*: quite; *śanaiḥ:* slowly; *na*: not; *vegataḥ*: quickly; *pūrya*: having inhaled; *piṅgalayā*: through the right nostril; *punaḥ*: again; *pūrayet*: he should fill; *śanaiḥ*: slowly; *udaram*: inner area.

Translation

Then, having closed his right nostril with the thumb of his right hand, he should inhale very slowly through the left nostril, and then, without pausing, he should perform breath retention for as long as he can. He should exhale again through the right nostril quite slowly, not quickly. Having inhaled through the right nostril again, he should slowly fill the inner area.

Commentary

Having offered *praṇam,* or respectful greeting, to one's iṣṭa devata, the practitioner begins the yoga practice with prāṇāyāma. The prāṇāyāma technique prescribed here is *nāḍī śodhana*, the breath balancing practice. This was the major method that the ancient yogis used as a preliminary to meditation. Holding the right hand in front of the face, the right nostril should be closed with the pressure of the thumb. One should then inhale very slowly through the left nostril. At the end of inhalation, one should perform *kumbhaka*, internal breath retention, for as long as possible.

In this verse the left and right nostrils are referred to as *iḍā* and *piṅgalā*. Iḍā is the flow of lunar or mental energy, which passes through the left nostril. Piṅgalā is the flow of solar or vital energy, which passes through the right nostril. The purpose of balancing the breath is to balance these two flows of energy. The practice of kumbhaka, internal breath retention, activates *suṣumnā*, the spiritual flow of energy. In order for meditation to be successful, it is necessary to first balance the breath, which controls the mental and vital energies, and then activate suṣumnā, the spiritual force.

One round of nāḍī śodhana prāṇāyāma equals two complete breaths. So, after inhaling through the left nostril and holding the breath inside, one should exhale through the right nostril. The speed of exhalation is emphasised here. The breath should be exhaled quite slowly, and not quickly, which would be the normal tendency, after holding the breath inside for as long as possible. After all the air has been expelled from the right nostril, the second half of the round begins. Now one should inhale again through the right nostril. Breathing in slowly, one should fill the lungs slowly to capacity.

Verse 39: Continuation of nāḍī śodhana prāṇāyāma

धारयित्वा यथाशक्ति रेचयेदिदया शनैः ।
यया त्यजेत्तयापूर्य धारयेदविरोधतः ।।३९।।
dhārayitvā yathāśakti recayediḍayā śanaiḥ
yayā tyajettayāpūrya dhārayedavirodhataḥ (39)

Anvay
dhārayitvā: having retained; *yathā-śakti*: as long as possible; *recayet*: he should exhale; *śanaiḥ:* slowly; *iḍayā*: through the left nostril; *yayā*: through whichever; *tyajet*: he exhales; *pūrya*: inhaling; *tayā*: through it; *dhārayet*: he should retain; *avirodhataḥ*: without interruption.

Translation
Having retained [the breath for] as long as possible, he should exhale slowly through the left nostril. Through whichever nostril he exhales, inhaling [again] through it, he should retain [the breath] without interruption.

Commentary
After inhaling through the right nostril, one should again retain the breath inside for as long as possible, without causing any distress or discomfort. Then the breath should be exhaled slowly through the left nostril. This completes one full round of nāḍī śodhana prāṇāyāma. In the first half of the round, one inhales through the left nostril and exhales through the right. In the second half, one inhales through the right nostril and exhales through the left. This process equalises the flow of breath in both the left and right nostrils, which in turn regulates the iḍā and piṅgalā nāḍīs, the parasympathetic and sympathetic nervous system and the right and left hemispheres of the brain.

The verse further explains that the inhalation should always follow through whichever nostril one exhales from. Further, the breath should always be retained immediately after each inhalation. In this way the practice may be continued for a number of rounds seamlessly. Retention of the breath, as described here is an important aspect of this practice, as it activates the suṣumnā nāḍī and the central nervous system, unifying the two hemispheres of the brain. The effects of this practice on the nervous system, the pranic system and the brain, make it an important requisite for meditation and all higher sādhanas.

Verse 40: How to regulate the duration of each breath

जानु प्रदक्षिणीकृत्य न द्रुतं न विलम्बितम् ।
अङ्गुलिस्फोटनं कुर्यात्सा मात्रा परिगीयते ।।४०।।
jānu pradakṣiṇīkṛtya na drutaṃ na vilambitam
aṅgulisphoṭanaṃ kuryātsā mātrā parigīyate (40)

Anvay
sā: this; *parigīyate*: is declared; *mātrā*: unit of time; *pradakṣiṇī*: to the right; *kṛtya*: to be made; *jānu*: on the knee; *na . . . na*: neither . . . nor; *drutam*: quickly; *vilambitam*: slowly; *sphotanam kuryāt*: he should snap; *aṅguli*: thumb.

Translation
This is declared: the *mātrā*, unit of time, [is measured] by making [a circle] to the right [with the hand] on the knee, neither quickly nor slowly, [and then] he should snap his thumb.

Commentary
The length of each breath can be regulated simply by counting, which is how most people practise prāṇāyāma today. However, counting becomes irregular in nāḍī śodhana, where there are two complete breaths in and out per round, plus retention after each inhalation. So, the yogis of old evolved this system to regulate the counting. The *mātrā*, or unit of time for each breath, was regulated by a particular hand movement.

During the practice of nāḍī śodhana, the right hand is raised in front of the face, so that the flow of breath can be directed in and out of each nostril by the pressure of the fingers. The left hand remains on the knee and is used to regulate the duration of the breath. First a circle is made with the left hand, rotating to the right and around to the left in a controlled way, neither too quickly nor too slowly. Upon completion of the circle, one should snap the fingers by bringing the thumb and middle finger together with adequate pressure.

Verses 41 and 42: Recommended ratio for nāḍī śodhana

इडया वायुमारोप्य शनैः षोडशमात्रया ।
कुम्भयेत्पूरितं पश्चाच्चतुः षष्ट्या तु मात्रया ।।४१।।
रेचयेत्पिङ्गलानाड्या द्वात्रिशन्मात्रया पुनः ।
पुनः पिङ्गलयापूर्य पूर्ववत्सुसमाहितः ।।४२।।
iḍayā vāyumāropya śanaiḥ ṣoḍaśamātrayā
kumbhayetpūritaṃ paścāccatuḥ ṣaṣṭyā tu mātrayā (41)
recayetpiṅgalānāḍyā dvātriśanmātrayā punaḥ
punaḥ piṅgalayā pūrya pūrvavatsusamāhitaḥ (42)

Anvay
iḍayā: through the left nostril; *vāyum*: air; *āropya*: having directed; *śanaiḥ*: slowl; *ṣoḍaśa*: sixteen; *mātrayā*: *mātrās*; *kumbhayet*: he should retain; *paścāt*: then; *pūritam*: fully; *ṣaṣṭyā*: sixty; *catuḥ*: four; *mātrayā*: *mātrās*; *recayet*: he should exhale; *punaḥ*: again; *piṅgalānāḍyā*: through the right nostril; *Dvaatrishan*: thirty two; *mātrayā*: *mātrās*; *pūrya*: having inhaled; *piṅgalayā*: through the right nostril; *punaḥ*: again; *pūrvavat*: as before; *susamāhitaḥ*: established.

Translation
Having directed the inhaled breath slowly through the left nostril for sixteen mātrās, he should then retain [the breath] fully for sixty four mātrās. He should exhale again through the right nostril for thirty two mātrās. Having inhaled again through the right nostril as before [he should become] established [in the practice].

Commentary
Here the recommended ratio, or number of mātrās, for the practice of nāḍī śodhana prāṇāyāma is given as a guideline for the practitioner. This may be considered as an advanced ratio to be used by one who has mastered the initial stages of

the practice. The practitioner should first inhale slowly through the left nostril for a duration of sixteen mātrās. Next the breath should be retained inside fully for a period of sixty four mātrās, and then exhaled through the right nostril for the duration of thirty two mātrās.

So, inhalation for sixteen mātrās, retention for sixty four matras, and exhalation for thirty two mātrās, makes the ratio of 1:4:2. It must be remembered that this ratio is not the initial practice. Much training and practice are required to develop sufficient lung capacity for this ratio to be performed with comfort and ease. The same ratio is to be followed for both breaths, first breathing in from the left nostril and out the right, and again breathing in through the right nostril and out the left, as described in the previous verses.

Verse 43: Number of practice sessions and rounds

प्रातर्मध्याम्दिने सायमर्धरात्रे च कुम्भकान् ।
शनैरशीतिपर्यन्तं चतुर्वारं समभ्यसेत् ।।४३।।
prātarmadhyāmdine sāyamardharātre ca kumbhakān
śanairaśītiparyantaṃ caturvāraṃ samabhyaset (43)

Anvay
samabhyaset: he should practise; *caturvāram*: four times; *dine*: a day; *prātar*: in the morning; *madhyām*: at midday; *sāyam*: in the evening; *ca*: and; *ardharātre*: at midnight; *śanaiḥ*: slowly; *paryantam*: up to; *aśīti*: eighty; *kumbhakān*: breath retentions.

Translation
He should practise four times a day: in the morning, at midday, in the evening and at midnight, slowly [increasing] up to eighty breath retentions.

Commentary
After establishing the practice, it is recommended for the serious sādhaka to perform the practice four times a day. Such an intensive practice is not intended for casual practitioners. It can only be undertaken by a person, who is able to set aside all worldly concerns for a period of time. The four optimal times in the day for this practice are also given here: (i) in the early morning around dawn, between 4:00 and 6:00 am, (ii) at midday from 11:00 am to 1:00 pm, (iii) in the early evening around dusk from 4:00 to 6:00 pm, and (iv) at midnight from 11:00 pm to 1:00 am. The number of rounds to be practised during each session is also given here. One should slowly work up to eighty breath retentions, or forty rounds.

Verses 44 and 45: Benefits of the practice of nāḍī śodhana

एवं मासत्रयाभ्यासान्नाडीशुद्धिस्ततो भवेत् ।
यदा तु नाडीशुद्धिः स्यात्तदा चिह्नानि बाह्यत: ।।४४।।
जायन्ते योगिनो देहे तानि वक्ष्याम्यशेसतः ।
शरीरलघुता दीप्तिर्जाठराग्निविवर्धनम् ।।४५।।
evaṃ māsatrayābhyāsānnāḍīśuddhistato bhavet
yadā tu nāḍīśuddhiḥ syāttadā cihnāni bāhyataḥ (44)
jāyante yogino dehe tāni vakṣyāmyaśeṣataḥ
śarīralaghutā dīptirjāṭharāgnivivardhanam (45)

Anvay
evam: in this way; *traya*: three; *māsa*: months; *abhyāsāt*: after the practice; *bhavet*: there should be; *tataḥ*: then; *śuddhiḥ*: purification; *nāḍī*: of the channels of energy; *yadā*: when; *syāt*: there is; *śuddhiḥ*: purification; *nāḍī*: of the energy channels; *tadā*: then; *bāhyataḥ*: external; *cihnāni*: signs; *jāyante*: are produced; *dehe*: in the body; *yoginaḥ*: of the yogi; *vakṣyāmi*: I shall describe; *tāni*: them; *aśeṣataḥ*: fully; *laghutā*: lightness; *śarīra*: of the body; *dīptih*: radiance; *vivardhanam*: increase; *jāṭhara-agni*: of digestive fire.

Translation
After practising in this way for three months, there should then be purification of the nāḍīs. When there is purification of the nāḍīs, then external signs are produced in the body of the yogin. I shall describe them fully: lightness of the body, radiance, increase of digestive fire.

Commentary
Here the results of the practice are given. If nāḍī śodhana is performed for three months, according to the method described above, the nāḍīs, or energy channels in the body,

will be purified. Purification of the nāḍīs is one of the important requisites for all the higher yogas. When the nāḍīs are purified, certain external signs manifest in the body. The first is lightness of the body, the second is radiance or luminosity, and the third is increased digestive power. These three qualities are also the signs of a yogi, one who has become adept in the practice of yoga.

Verse 46: Leanness of the body and choice of food

कृशत्वं च शरीरस्य तदा जायेत निश्चितम् ।
योगविघ्नकराहारं वर्जयेद्योगवित्तमः ।।४६।।
kṛśatvaṃ ca śarīrasya tadā jāyeta niścitam
yogāvighnakarāhāram varjayedyogavittamaḥ

Anvay
ca: and; *tadā*: then; *niścitam*: surely; *jāyeta*: it should bring about; *kṛśatvam*: leanness; *śarīrasya*: of the body; *yoga-vittamaḥ*: one who is accomplished in yoga; *varjayet*: should avoid; *āhāram*: food; *yoga-vighnakara*: obstructs yoga.

Translation
And then it should surely bring about leanness of the body. One who is accomplished in yoga should avoid foods [which] obstruct [the practice of] yoga.

Commentary
The yogi generally has a lean body. Mastery of the yogic practices, particularly nāḍī śodhana prāṇāyāma, rebalances the bodily systems. The nervous, metabolic and digestive systems function more efficiently and there is less buildup of toxin, fluid and fat in the body. The scriptural texts describe the yogi as one who is lean as a bamboo pole.

Again, having developed a certain mastery of yoga, one naturally becomes very careful in regard to diet. Wrong eating habits are counter-productive to yoga practice. A major aim of yoga is to purify and rebalance the body, so that spiritual awakening can take place. The body is comprised of the food one eats. Heavy, fatty, spicy and salty foods disturb the digestive system. They remain in the stomach for many hours and obstruct the practice of yoga during that period and even for long hours afterwards.

According to yoga, there are three types of diet: tamasic, rajasic and sattwic. Tamasic diet is comprised of foods, which are heavy, stale and old. These foods provide minimal energy and nutrients, and tend to clog the system. The preserved foods available in the supermarkets today are in this category. Rajasic diet contains foods, which are tasty, spicy, sour, pungent and salty. The fast food industry thrives on the production of this type of food, which today has become so addictive to the youth of every country. The combination of tamasic and rajasic diet is responsible for disease and suffering.

Sattwic diet is balancing, nutritious, light and bland. It is comprised of foods, which are fresh and produced locally in season. It is free from preservatives, pesticides and chemicals. Sattwic food digests very rapidly and leaves no toxic residues in the system. This diet is considered to be most appropriate for the practitioner of yoga, so it is also known as yogic diet.

Verses 47, 48 and 49: Guidelines during periods of practice

लवणं सर्षपं चाम्लमुष्णं रूक्षं च तीक्ष्णकम् ।
शाकजातं रामठादि वह्निस्त्रीपथसेवनम् ।।४७।।
प्रातः स्नानोपवासादिकायक्लेशांश्च वर्जयेत् ।
अभ्यासकाले प्रथमं शस्तं क्षीराज्यभोजनम् ।।४८।।
गोधूममुद्गशाल्यन्नं योगवृद्धिकरं विदुः ।
ततः परं यथेष्टं तु शक्तः स्याद्वायुधारणे ।।४९।।
lavaṇaṃ sarṣapaṃ cāmlamuṣṇaṃ rūkṣaṃ ca tīkṣṇakam
śākajātaṃ rāmaṭhādi vahnistrīpathasevanam (47)
prātaḥ snānopavāsādikāyakleśāṃśca varjayet
abhyāsakāle prathamaṃ śastaṃ kṣīrājyabhojanam (48)
godhūmamudgaśālyannaṃ yogavṛddhikaraṃ viduḥ
tataḥ paraṃ yatheṣṭaṃ tu śaktaḥ syādvāyudhāraṇe (49)

Anvay
varjayet: he should give up; *lavanam*: salt; *sarṣapam*: mustard; *ca*: and; *amlam*: sour; *uṣṇam*: hot; *rūkṣam*: dry; *tīkṣṇakam*: pungent; *śāka*: vegetables; *jātam*: of every kind; *rāmaṭha*: asafoetida; *ādi*: etc; *sevanam*: enjoyment of; *vahni*: fire; *strī*: women; *patha*: travel; *snāna*: bathing; *prātaḥ*: in the morning; *upavāsa*: fasting; *ādi*: etc; *ca*: and; *kāya-kleśān*: distress to the body; *kāle*: during the period; *abhyāsa*: of yoga practice; *bhojanam*: food; *kṣīra*: milk; *ājya*: ghee; *śastam*: is ordained; *prathamam*: the best; *godhūmam*: wheat; *udga*: horse beans; *śālyannam*: boiled rice; *viduḥ*: are known for; *yoga-vṛddhikaram*: development of yoga; *tataḥ*: then; *syāt*: he should be; *param*: most; *śaktaḥ*: capable; *vāyu-dhāraṇe*: suspension of breath; *yatheṣṭam*: as long as he wishes.

Translation
He should give up salt, mustard and [food which is] sour and hot, dry and pungent, vegetables of every kind, asafoetida

etc, enjoyment of [the warmth of] fire, women and travel, bathing in the morning, fasting etc, and [whatever gives] distress to the body. During the period of yoga practice, food of milk and ghee is ordained the best. Wheat, horse beans and boiled rice are known for their development of yoga. Then he should be most capable of suspension of the breath for as long as he wishes.

Commentary

Here the specific condiments to be avoided by yogic practitioners are mentioned, such as mustard and asafoetida. Foods that are salty, sour, pungent, and dry are also included, along with vegetables of every kind. All of these items, with the exception of vegetables, fall into the rajasic category, which stimulates taste and desire. Yogis preferred a sattwic diet, which is bland and easily digested. Vegetables are generally considered to be sattwic, but are also not recommended here, because they contain large amounts of fibre. During periods of sadhana, small amounts of food would be consumed at one time, filling the stomach to only one half of its capacity. Therefore, the preferred foods were more concentrated and rich in carbohydrate, protein and fat.

Along with the dietary restrictions, the sincere yogi is further advised to give up all attachment to bodily comfort, the first and foremost being the warmth of the hearth and home. The body's sensitivity to heat and cold is a great deterrent in yoga. The yogi is therefore encouraged to develop equanimity in regard to heat and cold, so that the practice can continue without interruption. The second comfort to be given up is a partner of the opposite sex. Sexual relationships require time and energy, both of which need to be redirected towards the practice of yoga. They also cause emotional disturbance, which unsettles the mind and makes the deeper stages of yoga inaccessible.

Furthermore, fasting is to be given up, along with bathing in the early morning, and any activity that causes distress to the body. Too much fasting weakens the body and causes the mind to lose focus. The yogi is therefore recommended to take a sattwic diet, and to eat in moderation, not too much and not too little. In regard to bathing, the early morning hours are not advised, as the outside temperature drops at that time. The inner body temperature also drops due to the previous hours of sleep. Yogis generally take cold water bath, which is very refreshing and revitalises the system. But a cold bath in the early morning will cause distress to the body. Therefore, bathing should be done just before noon, when the sun is high in the sky and the body is warm.

Travel is also mentioned here as an activity to be given up during periods of sādhana, as it causes distress to the body. The very thought of a trip in the distant or near future is enough to disturb the mind. When travel is imminent, the mind constantly engages in the possibilities of what should be done and what will arise. Once the thought of travel takes hold of the mind, it becomes restless and difficult to focus on sādhana and meditation for any period of time. During the actual period of travel, the body is further subjected to many changes in the environment, climate, food, water and air. All these changes cause distress to the body and mind, making sādhana nearly impossible.

During the period of yoga practice, the following foods are recommended: dishes prepared with milk and clarified butter were considered to be the best, as they were highly nourishing and digestible. Intensive practice of prāṇāyāma raises the metabolic fire and burns the fat in the body. The natural fats found in dairy products help to maintain the metabolic balance. We must also consider that in times past, cows were carefully tended in the home and hermitage. All dairy products were consumed in their pure and fresh state, without any chemicals or pasteurization. Wheat bread, prepared without any yeast or raising additive, beans and boiled rice were also considered to be beneficial for the development of yoga.

The yogi, who observes these guidelines, should then be able to retain the breath for as long as he wishes. Here we should recall the basic ratio for the practice of nāḍī śodhana was 1:4:2. One should inhale for the count of 16, hold the breath for the count of 64 and exhale for the count of 32. This practice is very difficult to sustain, unless the body is perfectly balanced and finely tuned. Retention of the breath is a major practice for bringing about a spiritual awakening. It stills the body and mind, awakens the suṣumnā nāḍī and aids in expansion of consciousness.

Verses 50 and 51a: Kevala kumbhaka—spontaneous breath retention

यथेष्टधारणाद्वायोः सिध्येत्केवलकुम्भकः ।
केवले कुम्भके सिद्धे रेचपूरविवर्जिते ।।५०।।
न तस्य दुर्लभं किंचित् त्रिषु लोकेषु विद्यते ।५१।
yatheṣṭadhāraṇādvāyoḥ sidhyetkevalakumbhakaḥ
kevale kumbhake siddhe recapūravivarjite (50)
na tasya durlabhaṃ kiṃcit triṣu lokeṣu vidyate (51a)

Anvay

kevala kumbhaka: spontaneous breath retention; *sidhyet*: is attained; *dhāraṇāt-vāyoḥ*: by holding the breath in; *yatheṣṭa*: as long as possible; *siddhe*: when perfected; *kevale kumbhake*: in spontaneous breath retention; *reca*: exhaling; *pūra*: inhaling; *vivarjite*: are given up; *vidyate*: there exists; *na . . . kiṃcit*: nothing; *durlabham*: unattainable; *tasya*: by him; *triṣu*: in the three; *lokeṣu*: worlds.

Translation

Kevala kumbhaka, spontaneous breath retention, is attained by holding the breath inside for as long as possible. When perfected in spontaneous breath retention, exhaling [and] inhaling are given up. There exists nothing unattainable by him in the three worlds.

Commentary

In the previous verses the method of nāḍī śodhana prāṇāyāma was described. This method focuses on the ratio of breath through the alternate nostrils with the addition of kumbhaka, breath retention, at the end of each inhalation. Nāḍī śodhana was the main prāṇāyāma practised earlier, and it remains so even today, because of its balancing effects on the prāṇas, nervous system, and mind. The perfection of nāḍī śodhana is kevala kumbhaka, spontaneous breath retention, in which there is complete cessation of the breath for a period of time.

Cessation of the breath is an important stage of yoga, because it allows the deeper states of consciousness to be accessed effortlessly. When the breath stops, the mind becomes absolutely still. In this state of total stillness, the yogi is able to penetrate the subconscious and unconscious states. The active mind is the barrier to achieving in-depth meditation. When the mind is stilled as a result of kevala kumbhaka, meditation dawns effortlessly.

The verse further states that for the yogi, who is able to access the three states of consciousness through the attainment of kevala kumbhaka, spontaneous breath retention, nothing remains unattainable in the three worlds. The three states of consciousness: conscious, subconscious and unconscious, which can be accessed during spontaneous breath retention, are related to the three planes of existence: earthly, intermediary or purgatory, and heavenly.

Verses 51b, 52 and 53a: Three stages of kumbhaka

प्रस्वेदो जायते पूर्वं मर्दनं तेन कारयेत ।।५१।।
ततो ऽपि धारणाद्वायोः क्रमेणैव शनैः ।
कम्पो भवति देहस्य आसनस्थस्य देहिनः ।।५२।।
ततो ऽधिकतराभ्यासाद्दार्दुरी स्वेद जायते ।५३।
prasvedo jāyate pūrvaṃ mardanaṃ tena kārayet (51b)
tato 'pi dhāraṇādvāyoḥ krameṇaiva śanaiḥ
kampo bhavati dehasya āsanasthasya dehinaḥ (52)
tato 'dhikatarābhyāsāddārdurī sveda jāyate (53a)

Anvay
pūrvam: at first; *prasvedaḥ*: perspiration; *jāyate*: is produced; *tena*: therefore; *mardanam kārayet*: it should be cleaned; *tataḥ*: then; *api*: again; *krameṇa*: in the course of; *śanaiḥ*: slowly; *dhāraṇāt-vāyoḥ*: holding the breath; *dehinaḥ*: person; *bhavati*: has; *kampaḥ*: tremor; *dehasya*: in the body; *āsanasthasya*: while sitting; *tataḥ*: then; *adhikatara-abhyāsāt*: from much more practice; *dārdurī*: frog-like; *sveda*: sweat; *jāyate*: is produced.

Translation
At first perspiration is produced; therefore it should be cleaned. Then again, in the course of slowly holding the breath, the person experiences tremor in the body, while sitting. Then, from much more practice, frog-like sweat is produced.

Commentary
During the practice of kumbhaka, the yogi will experience different stages, which can be known by the signs that are given in this verse. In the first stage the yogi will perspire profusely, and the perspiration will need to be wiped off with

a clean cloth in-between the rounds of practice. Perspiration is an indication that the inner body temperature is increasing, due to activation of the yogic fire at the manipura cakra, or navel centre. The yogic fire is responsible for purification and transformation of the gross bodily elements into subtle essence.

In the second stage, while holding the breath for longer durations, the yogi experiences tremor in the body. This indicates the awakening of prāṇa śakti at anahata cakra, the heart centre, which rules the air element, or prāṇa vāyu. Then, from much longer practice, the third stage of kumbhaka is realized. This is indicated by a cold, or frog-like, sweat, which is produced during the practice, indicating the activation of viśuddhi cakra, the centre of purification and gateway to higher consciousness. So, first there is heat and then tremor. Finally, when the heat cools and the tremors abate, there is cold sweat. These are the signs of the first three stages of kumbhaka.

Verses 53b, 54 and 55: Levitation in kumbhaka

यथा च दर्दुरो भाव उत्प्लुत्योत्प्लुत्य गच्छति ।।५३।।
पद्मासनस्थितो योगी तथा गच्छति भूतले ।
ततो ऽधिकतराभ्यासाद्भूमित्यागश्च जायते ।।५४।।
पद्मासनस्थ एवासौ भूमिमुत्सृज्य वर्तते ।
अतिमानुषचेष्टादि तथा सामर्थ्यमुद्भवेत् ।।५५।।
yathā ca darduro bhāva utplutyotplutya gacchati (53b)
padmāsanasthito yogī tathā gacchati bhūtale
tato 'dhikatarābhyāsādbhūmityāgaśca jāyate (54)
padmāsanastha evāsau bhūmimutsṛjya vartate
atimānuṣaceṣṭādi tathā sāmarthyamudbhavet (55)

Anvay
ca: and; *yathā*: just as; *darduraḥ*: frog; *gacchati*: moves; *bhāva*: up; *utplutyotplutya*: by leaps and bounds; *tathā*: thus; *yogī*: yogi, adept in yoga; *gacchati*: moves; *sthitaḥ*: seated; *padmāsana*: lotus pose; *bhūtale*: on the ground; *tataḥ*: then; *adhikatara-abhyāsat*: because of much more practice; *tyagaḥ*: rising up; *bhūmi*: earth; *jāyate*: is accomplished; *ca*: and; *asau*: that person; *utsṛjya*: having levitated; *bhūmi*: earth; *vartate*: remains; *eva*: still; *padmāsanastha*: seated in *padmāsana*; *tathā*: thus; *sāmarthyam*: power; *atimānuṣa*: superhuman; *ceṣṭa*: action; *ādi*: and other things; *udbhavet*: may arise.

Translation
And, just as the frog moves up by leaps and bounds, thus the yogin moves [while] seated in padmāsana on the ground. Then, because of much more practice, rising up [from] the earth is accomplished, and that person, having levitated from the earth, still remains seated in padmāsana. Thus the power for superhuman action and other things may arise.

Commentary
In this verse the stages of kumbhaka are further described. In

the fourth stage, the breath retention becomes more effortless and spontaneous. The body feels very light, as if it were about to lift off the ground, even while seated in the meditative asana. This is another reason why padmāsana was chosen as the ideal posture for advanced practices of prāṇāyāma and meditation. Many of the āsanas were performed simply to loosen the limbs and strengthen the back, so that this posture could be maintained for long durations of time. Padmāsana is a locked posture in which the body will remain balanced, firm and steady, even if it rises off the ground, or the practitioner falls into a deep trance.

Here the teaching continues with the analogy of the frog. Just as the frog moves forward by leaps and bounds, the body begins to jerk and lift upward by its own momentum. Even while seated in padmāsana on the ground, the practitioner feels that the body is bounding upward. In the fifth stage, which follows after much more practice, the body actually rises from the ground. While levitating above the ground, the body remains seated in padmāsana. In this way the siddhis, or perfections of yoga, begin to manifest.

Lightness of the body is one of the eight siddhis, or paranormal yogic powers, which were experienced by the perfected yogins of old.

Verse 56: Importance of secrecy

न दर्शयेच्च सामर्थ्यं दर्शनं वीर्यवत्तरम् ।
स्वल्पं वा बहुधा दुःखं योगी न व्यथते तदा ।।५६।।
na darśayecca sāmarthyaṃ darśanaṃ vīryavattaram
svalpaṃ vā bahudhā duḥkhaṃ yogī na vyathate tadā (56)

Anvay
na darśayet: he should not reveal; *darśanam*: teaching; *sāmarthyam*: power; *vīry-avattaram*: heroically inspired; *tadā*: then; *yogī*: yogi, adept in *yoga*; *na*: not; *vyathate*: is affected; *duḥkham*: hardship; *svalpam*: very small; *vā*: or; *bahudhā*: great.

Translation
He should not reveal [this] teaching [whose] power [is] heroically inspired. Then the yogin is not affected by hardship, [whether] very small or great.

Commentary
When the fruits of yogic practice begin to manifest, one should not reveal them to others. All the yogic texts advocate absolute secrecy in regard to one's personal practice. One who keeps a box of gold and jewels in the house should not inform others about these assets and their whereabouts. In the same way, when the yogic practice begins to yield results, these experiences should not become a common topic for conversation. The practitioner who boasts and exclaims about the results of his or her practice will surely lose them. The results of the practice will steadily diminish and disappear altogether; in the same way that thieves will surely come in the dead of night to remove all the gold and jewels that are kept in the house of a foolish loud-mouth.

The verse speaks of the power of this teaching, as being heroically inspired. It means that such teaching was traditionally known only to a master yogin, who had realized the practice and its result for him or herself, and would reveal it only to a sincere and worthy practitioner. Such masters were considered to be heroes in their time, for they had attained the perfection of human birth and evolution through their practice.

It is further stated here that the realized yogin, who holds the practice and its results in secrecy and highest regard, will be empowered by it from within. In this way, he or she will experience an elevated life, free from suffering and the affects of all hardships, whether great or small.

Verses 57 and 58a: Physical effects of the practice

अल्पमूत्रपुरीषश्च स्वल्पनिद्रश्च जायते ।
कीलवो दूषिका लाला स्वेददुर्गन्धतानने ।।५७।।
एतानि सर्वथा तस्य न जायन्ते ततः परम् ।५८।
alpamūtrapurīṣaśca svalpanidraśca jāyate
kīlavo dūṣikā lālā svedadurgandhatānane (57)
etāni sarvathā tasya na jāyante tataḥ param (58a)

Anvay
alpa: little; *mūtra*: urine; *purīṣaḥ*: excrement; *jāyate*: are produced; *ca*: and; *svalpa*: very little; *nidraḥ*: sleep; *kīlavaḥ*: indeed; *dūṣikā*: rheum of the eyes; *lālā*: saliva; *sveda*: sweat; *dur-gandha*: bad smell; *tānane*: negligible; *tataḥ*: then; *param*: subsequently; *etāni*: these things; *na . . . sarvathā*: not at all; *jāyante*: arise; *tasya*: in him.

Translation
Little urine and excrement are produced, and [there is] very little sleep. [When] indeed, rheum of the eyes, saliva, sweat and bad smell are negligible, then subsequently these things do not arise in him at all.

Commentary
Now we are told of the physical effects, which manifest with mastery of the practice. First of all, the body of the yogin, who has mastered the higher stages of prāṇāyāma, will produce very small amounts of urine and faeces. This is because the metabolic processes will be purified and regenerated to the extent that whatever is consumed will be metabolized completely, leaving very little residue. The need for sleep will also be greatly reduced, as the practitioner enters into the deeper states of consciousness, even while awake, during the higher stages of the practice.

Similarly, the watery fluid that collects and streams from the eyes is greatly reduced. The secretion of saliva, sweat and body odour become negligible, and ultimately, they do not arise in the yogin at all.

Verses 58b, 59 and 60a: Power over the earth

ततो ऽधिकतराभ्यासाद्बलमुत्पद्यते बहु ।।५८।।
येन भूचर सिद्धिः स्याद्भूचराणां जये क्षमः ।
व्याघ्रो वा शरभो वापि गजो गवय एव वा ।।५९।।
सिंहो वा योगिना तेन मृचन्ते हस्तताडिताः ।६०।
tato 'dhikatarābhyāsādbalamutpadyate bahu (58b)
yena bhūcara siddhiḥ syādbhūcarāṇāṃ jaye kśamaḥ
vyāghro vā śarabho vāpi gajo gavaya eva vā (59)
siṃho vā yoginā tena mṛcante hastatāditāḥ (60a)

Anvay

tataḥ: then; *adhikatara-abhyāsāt*: after a lot more practice; *bahu*: great; *balam*: strength; *utpadyate*: arises; *yena*: by which; *syāt*: he attains; *bhūcara siddhiḥ*: power to move through earth, mountains and walls; *kśamaḥ*: gives the power; *jaye*: to have mastery over; *carāṇām*: creatures which move; *bhū*: on the earth; *tena*: thus; *vyāghraḥ*: tiger; *śarabhaḥ*: deer; *vā*: or; *api*: even; *gajaḥ*: elephant; *gavayaḥ*: wild bull; *mṛcante*: perish; *tāditāḥ*: struck; *hasta*: by the hand; *yoginā*: of the yogin.

Translation

Then, after a lot more practice, great strength arises, by which he attains *bhūcara siddhi*, which gives him the power to move through mountains and walls, and mastery over all creatures moving on the earth. Thus the deer, lion, tiger, or even elephant or wild bull perish, when struck by the hand of this yogin.

Commentary

After further practice, great physical strength arises. Such a yogi attains *bhūcara siddhi*, the power to walk the earth without fear of any living creature. By this power, the body is able to move anywhere on earth and to pass through walls and mountains. The body grows so powerful that any creature, such as a deer, lion, tiger, or even a wild bull or an elephant, will perish if struck by the hand of this yogin.

Verses 60b and 61: Power of attraction

कन्दर्पस्य यथा रूपं तथा स्यादपि योगिनः ।।६०।।
तद्रूपवशगा नार्यः काङ्क्षन्ते तसय सङ्गमम् ।
यदि सङ्गं करोत्येष तस्य बिन्दुक्षयो भवेत् ।।६१।।
kandarpasya yathā rūpaṃ tathā syādapi yoginaḥ (60b)
tadrūpavaśagā nāryaḥ kāṅkṣante tasya saṅgamam
yadi saṅgaṃ karotyeṣa tasya bindukṣayo bhavet (61)

Anvay
yoginaḥ: *yogin*; *syāt*: is; *api*: even; *yathā .. tathā*: just like; *rūpam*: form; *Kandarpasya*: Kāma, god of love; *nāryaḥ*: women; *vaśagāḥ*: enthralled by; *tadrūpa*: such an appearance; *kāṅkṣante*: desire; *sangamam*: intercourse; *tasya*: with him; *yadi*: if; *karoti*: he makes; *saṅgam*: connection; *eṣa*: then; *bhavet*: there will be; *kṣayaḥ*: decrease; *tasya*: of his; *bindu*: semen.

Translation
The *yogin* is just like the form of *Kāma*, the god of love. Women enthralled by such an appearance desire intercourse with him. If he makes [this] connection, then there will be a decrease of his semen.

Commentary
With the mastery of prāṇāyāma, the metabolic processes and the prāṇas remain elevated, giving the yogi an appearance of great beauty and luminosity. Hence he is said to resemble the form of Kāma, the god of love. Women are highly attracted to his beautiful appearance, like bees to honey, and immediately fall in love with him. However, if he indulges in sexual union with them, his semen will fall, and hence the level of prāṇa will decline.

Verse 62: Preservation of semen

वर्जयित्वा स्त्रियाः सङ्गं कुर्यादभ्यासमादरात् ।
योगिनो ऽङ्गे सुगन्धश्च जायते बिन्दुधारणात् ।।६२।।
varjayitvā striyāḥ saṅgaṃ kuryādabhyāsamādarāt
yogino 'ṅge sugandhaśca jāyate bindudhāraṇāt (62)

Anvay
varjayitvā: having given up; *saṅgam*: intercourse; *striyāḥ*: with woman; *kuryāt*: he should do; *abhyāsam*: practice; *ādarāt*: seriously; *dhāraṇāt*: by preserving; *bindu*: semen; *sugandhaḥ*: pleasant fragrance; *jāyate*: is produced; *aṅge*: in the body; *yoginaḥ*: of the yogin.

Translation
Having given up intercourse with woman, he should do [his] practice seriously. By preserving the semen, a pleasant fragrance is produced in the body of the yogin.

Commentary
Therefore, the yogi, who has attained a high level of mastery, should abstain from sexual intercourse with women, and remain dedicated to his practice. When the yogi is attracted towards the opposite sex and wishes to co-mingle, the mind and prāṇas become disturbed. In this condition of excitement and anticipation, it is difficult to maintain mental focus and clarity during the sādhana. When the semen is preserved, the prāṇa and mind of the yogi remain calm, and the body emits a pleasant fragrance.

Verse 63: Aum meditation

ततो रहस्युपाविष्टः प्रणवं प्लुतमात्रया ।
जपेत्पूर्वार्जितानां तु पापानां नाशहेतवे ।।६३।।
tato rahasyupāviṣṭaḥ praṇavaṃ plutamātrayā
japetpūrvārjitānāṃ tu pāpānāṃ nāśahetave (63)

Anvay
tataḥ: then; *upāviṣṭaḥ*: seated; *rahasi*: secret; *japet*: he should repeat; *praṇavam*: Aum; *pluta-mātrayā*: prolonged *mātrās*; *hetave*: for the purpose of; *nāśa*: destruction; *pūrvārjitānām*: previously committed; *pāpānām*: sins.

Translation
Then, seated in a secret [place], he should repeat *Aum* with prolonged mātrās for the purpose of the destruction of previously committed sins.

Commentary
Having mastered prāṇāyāma and attained the related powers, or siddhis, mentioned in the previous verses, the yogi should then sit in a quiet and secluded spot, which is not known to others, in order to practise the Praṇava. The creation has come into existence from the Prāṇa, universal energy. The Aum sound is known as Praṇava, because it is the first sound of creation. The Aum sound contains three syllables: 'A', 'U' and 'M'. The 'A sound corresponds to the conscious state. The 'U' sound corresponds to the subconscious state, and the 'M' sound to the unconscious state. When the Aum sound is repeated constantly with elongated 'A', 'U' and 'M' sounds, the three states of consciousness: waking, dreaming and sleeping, or conscious, subconscious and unconscious, are systematically awakened.

All the karmas, or actions, which one has done in this birth and previous births remain in seed form in the deeper consciousness. Aum, being the first sound, is the purest vibration. When this sound vibrates throughout the consciousness, it neutralizes and roots out all the karmas stored in the deeper layers of the consciousness.

Verse 64: First state of perfection

सर्वविघ्नहरो मन्त्र: प्रणव: सर्वदोषहा ।
एवमभ्यासयोगेन सिद्धिरारम्भसंभवा ।।६४।।
sarvavighnaharo mantraḥ praṇavaḥ sarvadoṣahā
evamabhyāsayogena siddhirārambhasaṃ bhavā (64)

Anvay
mantraḥ: subtle sound vibration; *praṇavaḥ*: Aum; *haraḥ*: destroys; *sarva*: all; *vighna*: obstacles; *hā*: removes; *doṣa*: faults; *evam*: in this way; *abhyāsa-yogena*: by the practice of yoga; *sambhavā*: he enters into; *ārambhasam*: first; *siddhiḥ*: supernatural accomplishment.

Translation
The mantra *Aum* destroys all obstacles [and] removes all faults. In this way, by the practice of yoga, he enters into the first *siddhi*.

Commentary
The obstacles and faults referred to in this verse are the weaknesses, which prevent one from succeeding in the path of yogic sādhana and meditation. These include: (i) disease, (ii) dullness, (iii) doubt, (iv) procrastination, (v) laziness, (vi) craving, (vii) erroneous perception, (viii) inability to achieve finer stages, and (ix) instability. When these obstructions are removed, the path of sādhana becomes unhindered. During the course of practice, different obstacles are bound to arise from time to time. For example, due to extensive introversion during periods of sādhana, the different systems of the body may be affected, causing physical ailments, relating to the digestive, respiratory, nervous or endocrine systems. Physical disorders may also manifest as an expression of purification.

Many times these obstructions relate with the influence of the *guṇas*, or qualities of nature. Ultimately, sādhana should lead one towards a state of *sattwa*, in which lightness and balance are experienced. However, there may be times when the sādhaka enters into the state of *tamas*, where heaviness and dullness arise, due to sitting in one place and position for extensive periods without sensory contact with the outside world. If tamas cannot be shaken, then the sādhaka may fall into habits of procrastination and laziness in regard to the practice. In this case, one would prefer to put the practice off until later, or maybe not perform it at all. Even when the practice is undertaken, one becomes lazy and is unable to apply oneself fully.

Again, when the sādhaka enters the state of *rajas,* the dullness experienced previously is replaced by desires and cravings for sensory objects, which are not conducive to the sadhana. These cravings distract the mind, and if the sādhaka gives way to them, there will be a break in the sādhana. If the sādhana is broken at any time, it may become very difficult to return to it.

Even when the sādhana proceeds well, sometimes erroneous perception may arise, especially when the practitioner has little previous experience of the deeper levels of sādhana and meditation. When one is unfamiliar with the inner states of mind and consciousness, psychic phenomena, such as visions and hallucinations, may become disturbing or frightening, making it difficult to continue the practice. Again, one may believe that one has achieved a high level of practice, when in fact, the reverse is true.

During the course of sādhana, it may also happen that even with regular and dedicated practice, one is unable to attain the finer or subtler states. One reaches a certain point, and then comes up against a mental curtain or wall, which is impossible to pass through. This obstruction can be very disheartening for the sādhaka, who has strong ambition and desire to attain the higher states. One requires much patience and strong resolution to continue the sādhana, even in the face of this obstruction, knowing that it will be lifted in the right time.

The last obstruction is instability, or inability to sit completely still during the practice. In meditation the body becomes restless or uncomfortable, and one is compelled to shift the position. The body may also shake or tremble involuntarily. This movement of the body prevents the practitioner from going deeper into the practice. Everytime the body moves, the mind is again thrown back into the conscious state. This instability indicates a disparity between the body and the mind, which needs to be addressed before the practitioner can proceed.

This verse states that all of the above obstructions can be removed by meditation on the mantra *Aum*. The obstructions arise due to a predominance of tamo and rajo guṇa at the time of sādhana. Aum is a pure sound vibration, which harmonizes the mind and consciousness, and brings about a sattwic state. By this yoga of meditation on the meaning of Aum, the symbol of Aum, and repetition of the sound of Aum, the sādhaka is able to progress, and so attains the first siddhi, or stage of perfection. In this stage, one is able to maintain the meditative state without disturbance of body or mind, and the sādhana thus becomes ongoing, steady and effortless.

Verses 65 and 66: Second state of perfection

ततो भवेद्घटावस्था पवनाभ्यासतत्परा ।
प्राणो ऽपानो मनो बुद्धिर्जीवात्मपरमात्मनोः ॥६५॥
अन्योन्यस्याविरोधेन एकता घटते यदा ।
घटावस्थेति सा प्रोक्ता तच्चिह्नानि ब्रविम्यहम् ॥६६॥
tato bhavedghaṭāvasthā pavanābhyāsatatparā
prāṇo 'pāno mano buddhirjīvātmaparamātmanoḥ (65)
anyonyasyāvirodhena ekatā ghaṭate yadā
ghaṭāvastheti sā proktā taccihnāni bravimyaham (66)

Anvay
tataḥ: then; *tatparā*: following upon that; *abhyāsa*: with practice; *pavana*: on the breath; *bhavet*: is; *ghaṭa avasthā*: second state; *yadā*: when; *ekatā*: union; *ghaṭate*: takes place; *anyonyasa*: with each other; *avirodhena*: without conflict; *prāṇaḥ*: upward-moving energy; *apānaḥ*: downward-moving energy; *manaḥ*: rational mind; *buddhiḥ*: intuitive mind; *jīvātma-paramātmanoḥ*: between the individual soul and the universal soul; *sā*: this; *proktā*: is declared; *ghaṭa avasthā*: second state; *aham*: I; *bravimi*: shall describe; *tat*: its; *cihnāni*: signs.

Translation
Then, following upon that, with practice on the breath, is the second state. When union takes place with each other without conflict, between *prāṇa* and *apāna*, *manas* and *buddhi*, *jīvātma* and *paramātma*, this is declared the second state. I shall describe its signs.

Commentary
The yogis practised prāṇāyāma as a form of meditation, because it helped them to jump over the mind and enter directly into the field of consciousness. After attaining the first state of perfection in yoga through repetition of and

meditation on *Aum*, prāṇāyāma should be taken up in order to attain the second state. The word *yoga* itself means 'union'. Here the union of yoga is described at three levels between: (i) prāṇa and apāna, (ii) manas and buddhi, and (iii) jīvātmā and paramātmā; or between energy, mind and spirit.

Yoga speaks of five prāṇas: (i) *prāṇa*, (ii) *apāna*, (iii) *samāna*, (iv) *udāna*, and (v) *vyāna*, which together maintain all of the physical systems and their functions. Each prāṇa has its own particular location and direction of flow in the body. Prāṇa and apāna are the two prāṇas, which flow upward and downward, thus maintaining the equilibrium of the body. Prāṇa flows upward in the region of the chest from the diaphragm to the shoulders. Apāna flows downward in the pelvic region from the waist to the pelvic floor. The inhalation relates with prāṇa and the exhalation with apāna. When the breath is regulated through the practice of prāṇāyāma, these two prāṇas unite at the solar plexis, bringing about an awakening of the kundalini, or spiritual force. This is the first level of union.

In yoga the mind is known as *antaḥkaraṇa*, or the 'inner instrument' of consciousness. The antaḥkaraṇa is comprised of four components: (i) *manas*, (ii) *buddhi*, (iii) *citta* and (iv) *ahaṃkāra*. Manas is the lower, thinking or rational mind, and buddhi is the higher faculty of intellect, awareness and discrimination.

Citta is the accumulation of memories or associations, which are stored in the consciousness, and ahaṃkāra is the ego or identification principle. Normally, most individuals are ruled by manas, the thinking component of mind, which is constantly influenced by the ego and the associations. Buddhi, the higher mind, or awareness principle, is less functional or non-functional in most people. With the awakening of energy, which results from the union of prāṇa and apāna, buddhi, the awareness principle awakens and unites with manas. Thus the thinking mind is suffused with awareness, wisdom and discrimination. This is the second level of union.

The third and highest level of union takes place between the *jīvātmā*, individual self, or conciousness, and the *paramātmā*, supreme or universal self or consciousness. The word *jiva* means 'living' and *ātmā* means 'self'. When the self, the atma, is born and lives in a human body, it is known as jivatma. The ātmā in itself is eternal and unbound, but when it is born in the body, it becomes limited by the physical constraints and thus bound by them. If the jīvātmā can be merged into the paramātmā, even while living, the outcome is *mokṣa*, self-realization or liberation. This is the ultimate union of yoga. The verse states that all three levels of union described above can be achieved through the practice of prāṇāyāma.

Verses 67 and 68a: Practice of prāṇāyāma

पूर्वं यः कथितोऽभ्यासश्चतुर्थांशं परिग्रहेत् ।
दिवा वा यदि वा सायं याममात्रं समभ्यसेत् ।।६७।।
एकवारं प्रतिदिनं कुर्यात्केवलकुम्भकम् ।६८।
pūrvaṃ yaḥ kathito 'bhyāsaścaturthāśaṃ parigrahet
divā vā yadi vā sāyaṃ yāmamātraṃ samabhyaset (67)
ekavāraṃ pratidinaṃ kuryātkevalakumbhakam (68a)

Anvay
parigrahet: he should undertake; *caturthāśam*: one fourth; *abhyāsaḥ*: practice; *kathitaḥ*: prescribed; *pūrvam*: before; *samabhyaset*: he should practise; *mātram*: only one; *yāma*: period of two hours; *yadi . . . vā*: either . . . or; *divā*: by day; *sāyam*: at night; *kuryāt*: he should do; *kevala kumbhakam*: spontaneous breath retention; *ekavāram*: once; *pratidinam*: every day.

Translation
He should undertake one fourth of the practice described before. He should practise only one restraint, either by day or at night. He should do *kevala kumbhaka* once every day.

Commentary
The practice of prāṇāyāma is explained in detail in verses 35-40. The process is described in verses 41-43, including the ratio, the number of practice sessions per day, and the duration of each practice session. These are general instructions, which can be found in different upaniṣads and classical yogic texts. In this verse, however, specific instructions are given for the practitioner. Initially, prāṇāyāma should be practiced one time only, either in the day or in the night. The practice should be performed for one *yama*, or a period of two hours. The verse further mentions *kevala kumbhaka*, spontaneous breath retention, and says that it should be done only once every day.

This means that one should practise for a period of two hours, or until spontaneous kumbhaka occurs. After the arising of kevala kumbhaka, there is no need to continue or repeat the practice.

Verses 68b, 69, 70, 71 and 72: Practice of pratyāhāra, sensory control

इन्द्रियाणीन्द्रियार्थेभ्यो यत्प्रत्याहरणं स्फुतम् ।।६८।।
योगी कुम्भकमास्थाय प्रत्याहारः स उच्यते ।
यद्यत्पश्यति चक्षुर्भ्यां तत्तदात्मेति भावयेत् ।।६९।।
यद्यच्छृणोति कर्णाभ्यां तत्तदात्मेति भावयेत् ।
लभते नासया यद्यत्तत्तदात्मेति भावयेत् ।।७०।।
जिह्वया यद्रसं ह्यत्ति तत्तदात्मेति भावयेत् ।
त्वचा यद्यत्स्पृशेद्योगी तत्तदात्मेति भावयेत् ।।७१।।
एवं ज्ञानेन्द्रियाणां तु तत्तत्सौख्यं सुसाधयेत् ।
याममात्रं प्रतिदिनं योगी यत्नादतन्द्रितः ।।७२।।
indriyāṇīndriyārthebhyo yatpratyāharaṇaṃ sphuṭam (68b)
yogī kumbhakamāsthāya pratyāhāraḥ sa ucyate
yadyatpaśyati cakṣurbhyāṃ tattadātmeti bhāvayet (69)
yadyacchṛṇoti karṇābhyāṃ tattadātmeti bhāvayet
labhate nāsayā yadyattattadātmeti bhāvayet (70)
jihvayā yadrasaṃ hyatti tattadātmeti bhāvayet
tvacā yadyatspṛśedyogī tattadātmeti bhāvayet (71)
evaṃ jñānendriyāṇāṃ tu tattatsaukhyaṃ susādhayet
yāmamātraṃ pratidinaṃ yogī yatnādatandritaḥ (72)

Anvay

yat: for; *pratyāharaṇam*: withdrawing; *sphutam*: completely; *indriyāṇī*: sense organs; *indriya-arthebhyaḥ*: from the objects of the senses; *āsthāya*: through strenuous; *kumbhakam*: retention of the breath; *sa*: this; *ucyate*: is called; *pratyāhāraḥ*: *pratyāhāra*; *yadyat*: whatever; *yogī*: *yogin*; *paśyati*: sees; *cakṣurbhyām*: with his eyes; *tat-tat*: then this; *bhāvayet*: is to be; *iti*: declared; *ātmā*: self, consciousness, spirit; *śṛnoti*: he hears; *karṇābhyām*: with his ears; *labhate*: he perceives; *nasayā*: through his nose; *rasam*: taste; *atti*: he eats; *jihvayā*: with his tongue; *spṛśet*: he touches; *tvacā*: with his skin; *evam*: thus; *yatnāt*: with effort; *atandritaḥ*: undaunted; *tat-tat-saukhyam*: for the welfare;

jñānendriyāṇām: of the sense organs; *susādhayet*: should control; *mātram*: for a period; *yāma*: two hours; *pratidinam*: every day.

Translation

Complete withdrawal of the sense organs from the objects of the senses by strenuous retention of the breath is called *pratyāhāra*. Whatever the yogin then sees with his eyes, this is to be declared ātman. Whatever he then hears with his ears, this is to be declared ātman. Whatever he then smells through his nose, this is to be declared ātman. Whatever he then tastes with his tongue, this is to be declared ātman. Whatever he then touches with his skin, this is to be declared ātman. Thus, with undaunted effort, for the welfare of the sensory organs, the yogin should control them for a period of two hours every day.

Commentary

Today prāṇāyāma is practised as a part of hatha yoga to balance the nervous system and increase the energy. However, the yogis of old practised prāṇāyāma as a means to meditation. This verse describes how the practice of vigorous breath retention leads directly to the state of *pratyāhāra*, introversion of the senses, which is the first stage of meditation described in rāja yoga. When the senses are completely withdrawn from the objects of the world and focused within the mind, the yogi perceives his own self, or ātman.

This verse describes the five senses and their action. Normally, a person sees the objects of the world through the eyes. hears the objects through the ears, smells the objects through the nose, tastes the objects through the tongue, and feels the objects through the skin. When all the five senses are projected outward in this way, one experiences the world, as if one were outside in it.

But this is an illusion. The experiences of the world are never outside; they are only reflections of the sensory organs, perceived in the mind. Therefore, the world is regarded as illusory, while the consciousness, or the self, is real.

While living in the world, a person generally becomes so accustomed to directing the senses outward, that one remains unaware of and unable to perceive one's own inner self. The yogis considered this condition of humankind to be deplorable. Even while living in the body and performing one's duties in life, a person should still be able to know oneself. Hence, the practices of yoga evolved, not just to live a better life, a more healthy life, but to know the self.

The yogi is a person, who practices with undaunted effort, for a long time, without giving up. A practitioner may easily become discouraged by the strenuous effort required and disappointed by the lack of an immediate result. The verse states that in order to attain pratyāhāra, the yogi should control the senses and direct them inwardly for a period of two hours every day. In this way, the senses and the mind will be purified and strengthened, so that one can enter the higher states of meditation.

Verses 73, 74 and 75: Siddhis or powers of yoga

यथा वा चित्तसामर्थ्यं जायते योगिनो ध्रुवम् ।
दूरश्रुतिर्दूरदृष्टिः क्षणाद्दूरागमस्तथा ।।७३।।
वाक्सिद्धिः कामरूपत्वमदृश्यकरणी तथा ।
मलमूत्रप्रलेपेन लोहादेः स्वर्णता भवेत ।।७४।।
खे गतिस्तसय जायेत संततताभ्यासयोगतः ।
सदा बुद्धिमता भाव्यं योगिना योगसिद्धये ।।७५।।
yathā vā cittasāmarthyaṃ jāyate yogino dhruvam
dūraśrutirdūradṛṣṭiḥ kṣaṇāddūrāgamastathā (73)
vāksiddhiḥ kāmarūpatvamadṛśyakaraṇī tathā
malamūtrapralepena lohādeḥ svarṇatā bhavet (74)
khe gatistasya jāyeta saṃtatābhyāsayogataḥ
sadā buddhimatā bhāvyaṃ yoginā yogasiddhaye (75)

Anvay

vā: just; *yathā*: as; *yoginaḥ*: yogin's; *sāmarthyam*: power; *citta*: of mind; *jāyate*: becomes; *dhruvam*: stable; *tathā*: then; *bhavet*: arises; *dūraśrutiḥ*: clairaudience; *dūradṛṣṭiḥ*: clairvoyance; *dūrāgamaḥ*: travel far; *kṣaṇāt*: within a moment; *Vaaksiddhih*: power of speech; *karaṇī*: ability to; *kāma-rūpatvam*: assume any form desired; *adṛśya*: become invisible; *lohādeḥ*: from iron; *pralepena*: smeared with; *mala*: excrement; *mūtra*: urine; *svarṇatā*: gold; *buddhimatā*: wise; *yoginā*: *yogin*; *bhāvyam*: must be; *sadā*: always; *yogataḥ*: assiduously; *saṃtata*: continuously; *abhyāsa*: practising; *yoga-siddhaye*: for attainment in *yoga*; *khe gatiḥ*: levitation; *jāyeta*: should be possible; *tasya*: for him.

Translation

Just as the *yogin*'s power of mind becomes stable, then arises clairaudience, clairvoyance, [the ability to] travel far within a moment, [great] power of speech, the ability to assume any form desired, [and] to become invisible, [and to turn] iron, [when] smeared with excrement and urine, into gold. The wise *yogin* must always be assiduously [and] continuously practising for attainment in yoga. [Then] levitation should be possible for him.

Commentary

This verse describes eight siddhis, or powers of perfection, which arise in the yogi, who practices continuously for a long period of time. Through regular practice, the distraction and dissipation of the mind gradually cease and the mind becomes stable. The mind is considered to be stable, when the yogi can remain focused within, on one point, without fluctuation, for an extended duration. When the mind becomes stable, the first perfection that arises is clairaudience, the ability to hear within. This ability makes it is possible to perceive within one's own mind what another is thinking or feeling, without any external interaction or input through the ears.

The second perfection is clairvoyance, the ability to see within. Inner vision allows the yogi to see any person, place, object or situation within his own mind, without any external contact through the eyes. The third perfection is the ability to astral travel, while the physical body remains inert in one place. The yogi is able to leave the physical body and travel in his subtle body to any destination in time and space within a moment, and then return to the physical body unhampered. The fourth perfection is the power of speech. The yogi will become a great orator, able to inspire multitudes. The words uttered by such a yogi are melodious, well spoken and bound to be true.

The fifth perfection is the ability to assume any form desired. This siddhi is mentioned in the ancient texts, but it is not seen today. It involves transforming one's present form into another form at will, and then changing it back to the original again. In the *Rāmacaritamānas,* the life story of Śri Rāma, who lived several thousand years ago, we find abundant references to this siddhi. For example, Hanumān, the great devotee of Śri Rāma, was born as a *Vanara*, a race of half monkey/ half man, but he could change his form at any time. When he first encountered Śri Rāma, he felt ashamed of his monkey form, and transformed himself into a Brahmin. But Śri Rāma saw into the deception, and when they embraced, Hanumān immediately resumed his monkey form.

The sixth perfection is the ability to become invisible. This siddhi is also not seen today, although sometimes we may wish we had it. It involves the ability to dematerialize one's physical form at any time or in any situation, and then to materialize it again at will. The seventh perfection is what achemists have sought to achieve from time immemorial. The ability to transform iron that is smeared with urine and feces into gold. Here iron, urine and feces represent the rough, gross forms of matter, while gold is the pure element. The eighth siddhi mentioned here is levitation, the ability to elevate the body without any external supports. This perfection arises in the yogi, who practises regularly and tirelessly, over a long period of time.

Verses 76, 77 and 78a: Siddhis are obstacles in yoga

एते विघ्ना महासिद्धेर्न रमेत्तेषु बुद्धिमान् ।
न दर्शयेत्स्वसामर्थ्यं यस्यकस्यापि योगिराट् ।।७६।।
यथा मूढो यथा मूर्खो यथा बधिर एव वा ।
तथा वर्तेत लोकस्य स्वसामर्थ्यस्य गुप्तये ।।७७।।
शिष्याश्च स्वस्वकार्येषु प्रार्थयन्ति न संशयः ।७८।
ete vighnā mahāsiddherna rametteṣu buddhimān
na darśayetsvasāmarthyaṃ yasya kasyāpi yogirāt (76)
yathā mūḍho yathā mūrkho yathā badhira eva vā
tathā varteta lokasya svasāmarthyasya guptaye (77)
śiṣyāśca svasvakāryeṣu prārthayanti na saṃśayaḥ (78a)

Anvay
ete: these; *mahāsiddheḥ*: great powers; *vighnāḥ*: obstacles; *buddhimān*: wise man; *na*: not; *ramet*: should delight; *teṣu*: in them; *yogirāt*: king of yogins; *na darśayet*: should not display; *sva-sāmarthyam*: his own ability; *yasyakasya-api*: to anyone whatsoever; *varteta*: he should live; *lokasya*: in the world; *yathā*: like; *mūḍhaḥ*: fool; *mūrkhaḥ*: idiot; *vā*: or; *eva*: even; *badhiraḥ*: deaf person; *tathā*: thus; *guptaye*: guarding; *sva-sāmarthyasya*: his own power; *na saṃśayaḥ*: no doubt; *śiṣyāḥ*: disciples; *prārthayanti*: would beg; *svasvakāryeṣu*: for their own purposes.

Translation
These great powers [are] obstacles. The wise man should not delight in them. The king of yogins should not display his own ability to anyone, whosoever. He should live in the world like a fool, an idiot or even a deaf person, thus guarding his own power. There is no doubt his disciples would beg [him to reveal his powers] for their own purposes.

Commentary
Although a worldly person may think of the above mentioned

siddhis as most desireable and advantageous, the yogi looks upon them as obstacles to the spiritual path. The aim of a yogi is nothing less then enlightenment, while living in the physical body, in this material world. Delving into the powers of yoga may prove to be a great distraction to the yogi and prevent him or her from attaining his goal in this very lifetime. Therefore, the wise yogi, who has attained the level of siddhi, never takes pleasure in such powers or exhibits them to others, no matter who they may be. If asked whether or not the yogi has attained such powers, he or she will deny it.

Not too long ago, there was a great siddha, living in the South of India. He stayed with a pack of mongrel dogs in a small hut outside the town, on the edge of a forest. After a while, the townspeople came to know that a siddha yogi was living nearby, and they came one day in a group to pay him a visit. As they were approaching the siddha's hut, he ran outside and quickly began to gather up a pile of rocks. When the people came within hearing range, he shouted at them, "Go away and never come back." But the people did not heed his words and continued walking towards him. So the siddha began to pelt them with the stones. He went on throwing stones at them, until they finally turned round and headed back to the town. Then he shouted, "Never come here again. If you do, I will set my dogs upon you."

It is further said here that the siddha yogi should not live as a great person. He or she should not expect or wish to be respected, praised or revered for having attained yogic powers. Rather, he or she should appear to others like a fool, an idiot or a mute. For it is only in this way that the yogic powers can be safe-guarded from exposure and use for worldly gain. It also stands to reason, and so the verse goes on to say that, otherwise the disciples of such a siddha would undoubtedly ask him again and again to show and then to give them these powers for their own worldly purposes.

Verses 78b and 79: Assiduous practice

तत्तत्कर्मकरव्यग्रः स्वाभ्यासे ऽविस्मृतो भवेत् ।।७८।।
अविस्मृत्य गुरोर्वाक्यमभ्यसेत्तदहर्निशम् ।
एवं भवेद्घठावस्था संतताभ्यासयोगतः ।।७९।।
tattatkarmakaravyagraḥ svābhyāse 'vismṛto bhavet (78b)
avismṛtya gurorvākyamabhyasettadaharniśam
evaṃbhavedghaṭhāvasthā saṃtatābhyāsayogataḥ (79)

Anvay
tat-tat: however; *vyagraḥ*: he who is occupied with; *karmakara*: working for others; *bhavet avismṛtaḥ*: should not forget; *sva-abhyāse*: his own practice; *avismṛtya*: not forgetting; *vākyam*: words; *guroḥ*: of the guru; *tad*: then; *abhyaset*: he should practise; *aharniśam*: day and night; *evam*: thus; *yogataḥ*: assiduously; *saṃtata*: continuously; *abhyāsa*: practising; *bhavet*: he becomes; *ghaṭha-avasthā*: second state.

Translation
However, he who is occupied with working for others should not forget his own practice. Not forgetting the words of the guru, then he should practise day and night. Thus, assiduously and continuously practising, he becomes (enters) the second state.

Commentary
The teaching given in this upaniṣad stresses the importance of assiduous practice. However, the path of yoga should not be followed in a selfish or obsessive way. If yoga is performed for oneself alone, the progress may be slow due to focus on and enhancement of the ego in relation to the practice. Therefore, the practitioner should always be mindful of the welfare and upliftment of others. At the same time, yogic aspirants, who are busy with work, family and social life, and have not yet attained siddhi, or

perfection, should be regular in their own personal practice. They should receive regular guidance from the guru, regarding their practice, and should follow this diligently. By following the advice of the guru and not forgetting his or her words, they will progress in the practice without being deterred by obstacles and difficulties.

Whenever the aspirant is free from work and family obligations, he or she should practise as much as possible, both in the day and at night. Through dedicated and regular practice, one attains the ghatha state. The word *ghaṭha* used here refers the second stage of yoga, where the awareness is able to penetrate and remain conscious in the subconscious state. Ghaṭha is a clay pot or jar that has been tempered by heat. The clay pot that has been fired in a kiln is able to retain water and other substances without subsequent leakage. Similarly, the sustained practice of yoga awakens the yogic fire in the aspirant, which gradually strengthens and transforms the body and mind into a vessel capable of withstanding the initial awakening of consciousness and energy that takes place during the second stage of yoga.

Verses 80 and 81a: Importance of associations and devotion

अनभ्यासवतश्चैव वृथागोष्ठ्या न सिद्ध्यति ।
तस्मात्सर्वप्रयत्नेन योगमेव सदाभ्यसेत् ।।८०।।
ततः परिचयावस्था जायते ऽभ्यासयोगतः ।८१।
anabhyāsavataścaiva vṛthāgoṣṭhyā na siddhyati
tasmātsarvaprayatnena yogameva sadābhyaset (80)
tataḥ paricayāvasthā jāyate 'bhyāsayogataḥ (81a)

Anvay
ca: and; *eva*: indeed; *na siddhyati*: he does not gain; *vṛthā-goṣṭhyā*: by useless company; *anabhyāsavataḥ*: neglect of practice; *tasmāt*: therefore; *abhyaset*: he should practise; *sadā*: always; *yogam*: yoga; *sarva-prayatnena*: with complete devotion; *tataḥ*: then; *abhyāsayogataḥ*: through strenuous practice; *paricaya-avasthā*: third state; *jāyate*: is attained.

Translation
And indeed, he does not gain by useless company [which leads to] neglect of practice. Therefore he should always practise yoga with complete devotion. Then, through strenuous practice, the third state (of yoga) is attained.

Commentary
The sincere yoga practitioner should avoid unneccessary association with persons, who are totally identified with the relationships and activities of the world, and have no interest in yoga or self-realization. The company of such persons on a casual or regular basis is counter-productive, because it distracts the mind and leads it away from the practice. The mind of a worldly person is more externalized, and requires constant engagement, distraction and entertainment. The yoga practitioner, on the other hand, is learning to disengage the mind from dependence on external associations, in order to focus the attention within.

This inner work requires a totally different kind of effort and awareness, and the practitioner may meet with obstacles on the path, which make it difficult to remain centered and progress. At times, he or she may feel isolated and alone, with no one to reach out to who understands. Therefore, it is important for the sincere practitioner to have a yoga *saṅgha*, or spiritual associations, who can understand and support his or her aspirations and practice. The yoga saṅgha is group of like-minded persons, who share similar ideals and practices, in the same way that different family, social or professional groups support and help to further one's activities in the world.

In order to develop an inner life and progress in one's practice, one needs a different peer group, different friends and associations, who think and live in a similar way and share similar life visions and goals. Coming together with this group is called *satsaṅg,* being in the company of truth. Satsaṅg is an important requisite for those who wish to follow the yogic path, and it is often mentioned in the yogic texts. By attending satsaṅg the practitioner develops firm faith and conviction in the path, and is able to practise with complete dedication and devotion. In the absence of devotion, the practitioner will inevitably lose interest and motivation, and the practice will become irregular.

Therefore, the verse says that one should always practise yoga with complete devotion, and in this way, the practice will become stronger and stronger. The quality or the feeling of devotion has a very powerful influence on the mind. When devotion is added to the practice, it acts as a kind of glue, allowing the mind to adhere to and continue with the practice over a long period of time, without dissipation or slackening of effort. Devotion also sweetens the practice, in the same way that the presence of a lover or beloved sweetens one's life in the external world. When the yoga practice is performed regularly with complete devotion, the mind becomes steady and unshakeable. Slowly the awareness penetrates deeper and deeper into the veils of consciousness until the *paricaya avasthā*, or third state of yoga, is attained, where the awareness remains conscious even in the unconscious state.

Verses 81b, 82 and 83a: Awakening of the kuṇḍalinī

वायु: परिचितो यत्नादग्निना सह कुण्डलीम् ।।८१।।
भावयित्वा सुषुम्नायां प्रविशेद्रिरोधत: ।
वायुना सह चित्तं च प्रविशेच्च महापथम् ।।८२।।
यस्य चित्तं स्वपवन: सुषुम्नां प्रविशेदिह ।८३।
vāyuḥ paricito yatnādagninā saha kuṇḍalīm (81b)
bhāvayitvā suṣumnāyāṃ praviśednirodhataḥ
vāyunā saha cittaṃ ca praviśecca mahaapatham (82)
yasya cittaṃ svapavanaṃ suṣumnāṃ praviśediha (83a)

Anvay
vāyuḥ: breath; *yatnāt*: after much effort; *bhāvayitvā*: having stimulated; *kuṇḍalīm*: spiritual energy; *saha*: with; *agninā*: fire; *paricitaḥ*: knowingly; *praviśet*: enters; *suṣumnāyām*: spiritual energy channel; *nirodhataḥ*: without interruption; *yasya*: when; *svapavanaḥ*: one's own vital energy; *praviśet*: enters; *citta*: consciousness; *saha vāyunā*: with the breath; *praviśet*: ascends; *iha*: hither; *mahāpatham*: great path; *suṣumnām*: channel of kuṇḍalinī.

Translation
The breath, after much effort, having stimulated the kuṇḍalinī with fire, knowingly enters the suṣumnā without interruption. When one's own vital energy enters the citta with the breath, it ascends hither the great path of the suṣumnā.

Commentary
In yoga, the awakening of consciousness is always preceded by the activation of kuṇḍalinī. Consciousness and energy are the two principles of creation. Kuṇḍalinī is the cosmic energy, which descends from the unmanifest into the manifest, and is responsible for the creation of all beings and

existence. In this sense, kuṇḍalinī is the Mother of creation, and she brings it all about by the transmutation of her own cosmic force into a number of elements, or *tattwas*, which comprise the building blocks of all material existence in its manifold forms. In this way, the kuṇḍalinī remains immaterial in herself, although she is the mother of all forms of existence from the universe, galaxies and stars, to the minerals, vegetables and creatures of every dimension and kind.

In human beings, the kuṇḍalinī force descends from the unmanifest into the manifest through the channel of suṣumnā, which is located at the center of the spinal column. As the kuṇḍalinī descends through the suṣumnā, she makes certain energy deposits along the way, which when combined become the core forcefield for our individual existence all through life. These energy deposits are called *cakra*, circles or fields of psychic energy. Each cakra holds a particular elemental energy necessary for the creation and maintenance of our human existence. There are six major cakras, located alongside the suṣumnā. Ajña cakra is located at the mid-brain and holds the energy of individual consciousness and mind. Viśuddhi cakra is located behind the throat-pit and holds the energy of space or ether. Anāhata cakra is located behind the heart and holds the energy of air. Maṇipura cakra is located behind the navel and holds the energy of fire. Swādhiṣṭhāna chakra is located at the tail bone and holds the energy of water, and mūlādhāra cakra is located at the pelvic floor and holds the energy of earth.

Having travelled all this way, from the unmanifest down into the manifest, and deposited all the necessary elemental energies for our creation, the kuṇḍalinī coils herself up in the energy of earth at the mūlādhāra cakra and goes to sleep. While she sleeps, we dream our life on earth, and she sustains it with her energy. This is the position until one fine day she begins to awaken and ascends the suṣumnā in the same way as she descended. This is what will happen in every individual over the long course of our human evolution. However, the yogis of old made an important discovery. They found that the kuṇḍalinī could be awakened during one lifetime by the practices of yoga. This verse is a concise summary of this discovery.

Prāṇāyāma is a yogic practice, which gives mastery over the life force through control of the breath. The breath also refers to the vital energy, or prāṇa śakti. Prāṇāyāma is one of the important ways to awaken the kuṇḍalinī, and has been used by yogis for this purpose. The practices of prāṇāyāma involve mastering different ratios of the inhalation and exhalation, as well as the retention of the breath, both inner and outer. These practices require strenuous effort over a long period of time in order to attain proficiency. When prāṇāyāma is mastered, the two major channels of iḍā and piṅgalā, which spiral upward alongside the suṣumnā in opposite directions, are regulated and awakened. Iḍā and piṅgalā represent the dual forces of prāṇa śakti and citta śakti, vitality and consciousness. The awakening of iḍā and piṅgalā ignites the yogic fire at the mūlādhāra cakra, and initiates the awakening of the kuṇḍalinī.

The awakening of kuṇḍalinī causes this spiritual force, which has lain dormant in the root cakra, to become conscious, in the same way that a person becomes conscious after awakening from a deep sleep. Hence the kuṇḍalinī knowingly or consciously enters the mouth of suṣumnā and begins to ascend. Due to the force of prāṇa that is released at the moment of awakening, kuṇḍalinī enters the suṣumnā without interruption. The kuṇḍalinī draws the vital force along with it, and merges with citta, the inner field of consciousness, along with the breath. In this way the kuṇḍalinı ascends the great path of suṣumnā.

Verses 83b and 84a: Permutation of the five elements

भूमिरापो ऽनलो वायुराकाशश्चेति पञ्चकः ॥८३॥
येषु पञ्चसु देवानां धारणा पञ्चधोच्यते ।८४।
bhūmirāpo 'nalo vāyurākāśaśceti pañcakaḥ (83b)
yeṣu pañcasu devānāṃ dhāraṇā pañcadhocyate (84a)

Anvay
iti: it is said; *pañcakaḥ*: there are five; *bhūmiḥ*: earth; *āpaḥ*: water; *analaḥ*: fire; *vāyuḥ*: air; *ca*: and; *ākāśaḥ*: ether; *yeṣu pañcasu*: in these five; *dhāraṇā*: attention; *devānām*: of the deities; *ucyate*: is said; *pañcadhā*: five-fold.

Translation
It is said there are five [elements]: earth, water, fire, air and ether. In these five the attention of the deities is said [to be] five-fold.

Commentary
In the previous commentary, it was explained how the five elements came into existence in relation to the evolution of the kuṇḍalinī and the cakras. The five elements in this sense are not substances, but energies. All beings in the material world, whether sentient or insentient, are comprised of the same five elemental energies: earth, water, fire, air and ether. Although these five elements are the same in everyone and everything, their proportions are very different. Even in our human species, we can see that some people are more earthy, while others are more fiery or airy. This varying proportion in the elements makes each person unique and special.

All matter is created through the five elements, which undergo a continuous process of permutation and combination. Even in relation to the individual elements themselves, the proportional makeup of each element forms the components of the other elements. In yogic philosophy this process is explained as follows. Each individual element is divided into two equal parts. The first part forms the pure elemental energy. The second part is again divided into four equal parts, i.e., one eighth of the whole element. Then the first half of each element is combined with one eighth of each of the other four elements. In this way, the permutation and combination of the elements takes place to create the diversity of life.

Hence, in the verse, it says that the attention of the deities in these five elements is five-fold. The word *deva* or deity is used in this context as all the elements of creation were associated with particular aspects of the divine in ancient times. This infers that behind the manifest creation, there is the unmanifest existence, from which it arises and receives continual support.

Verses 84b, 85, 86 and 87a: Pṛthivī dhāraṇā

पादादिजानुपर्यन्तं पृथिवीस्थानमुच्यते ।।८४।।
पृथिवी चतुरस्रं च पीतवर्णं लवर्णकम् ।
पार्थिवे वायुमारोप्य लकारेण समन्वितम् ।।८५।।
ध्यायंश्चतुर्भुजाकारं चतुर्वक्त्रं हिरन्मयम् ।
धारयेत्पञ्च घटिकाः पृथिवीजयमाप्नुयात् ।।८६।।
पृथिवीयोगतो मृत्युर्न भवेदस्य योगिनः ।८७।

pādādijānuparyantaṃ pṛthivīsthānamucyate (84b)
pṛthivī caturasnaṃ ca pītavarṇaṃ lavarṇakam
pārthive vāyumāropya lakāreṇa samanvitam (85)
dhyāyaṃścaturbhajākāraṃ caturvakraṃ hiraṇmayam
dhārayetpañca ghaṭikāḥ pṛthivījayamāpnuyāt (86)
pṛthivīyogato mṛtyurna bhavedasya yoginaḥ (87a)

Anvay

ucyate: it is said; *sthānam*: site; *pṛthivī*: *pṛthivī*, earth element; *ādi*: begins at; *pāda*: feet; *paryantam*: ends at; *jānu*: knees; *caturasnam*: square; *pīta*: yellow; *varṇam*: in colour; *varṇakam*: has the sound; *la*: *lam*, bīja mantra or seed sound of earth element and mūlādhāra cakra; *āropya*: directing; *vāyum*: breath; *pārthive*: within the area of the earth element; *samanvitam*: together with; *lakāreṇa*: sound *lam*; *dhyāmam*: meditating on; *bhajākāram*: performing worship; *catur caturvaktram*: four mouthed and faced one, ie Brahma; *hiraṇmayam*: golden; *dhārayet*: he should concentrate; *pañca ghaṭikāḥ*: two hours (5 x 24 minutes); *āpnuyāt*: he would obtain; *jayam*: victory; *pṛthivī*: earth; *mṛtyuḥ*: death; *bhavet*: is; *na*: not; *asya*: for this; *yoginaḥ*: yogin; *yogataḥ*: united with; *pṛthivī*: earth element.

Translation

It is said that the site of *pṛthivī*, the earth element, begins at the feet and ends at the knees. (The symbol for) pṛthivī is a yellow square, and the bīja mantra, or seed sound, is *lam*.

Directing the breath within the area of the earth element together with the sound *lam*, meditating on and performing worship to the four faced, golden one, he should concentrate for two hours. [Thus] he would obtain victory over the earth. Death is not for this yogin, who has united with the earth element.

Commentary

These verses describe the method of *pṛthivī dhāraṇā*, or meditation on the earth element. The location of the earth element in the physical body is in-between the knees and the toes. The symbol that invokes this energy is a large yellow square. Yellow is the color of earth and the square represents its solid and substantial nature. The bīja mantra, or seed sound, associated with this element is *lam*, which is also the sound for mūlādhāra cakra, located in the region of the pelvic floor. Although mūlādhāra cakra holds the initial store of pṛthivī energy, this element has its own location in the physical body, which is different to the cakra.

In order to meditate on the earth element, the practitioner should direct the awareness into the region between the knees and the toes and here visualize a large, heavy yellow square. Mentally trace the four sides of the large square. See the yellow color. Feel the solidity, the weight. Then add the breath, inhaling up one side, exhaling across the next side, inhaling down the third side and exhaling across the fourth side. The sound *lam* should be repeated with each inhalation and exhalation.

When the concentration deepens, and becomes spontaneous, begin to visualize the form of Brahma, the lord of creation. Brahma is of golden hue with four heads and four mouths. As in the yellow square, the four heads and four mouths represent the four directions on earth.

By meditating regularly in this way for a duration of two hours, the earth element will be purified and strengthened. The practitioner will gradually become one with the earth energy and will thus attain mastery over it. Death will not come unbidden to this yogi, who has united with the energy of the earth element.

Verses 87b, 88, 89 and 90: Āpas dhāraṇā

आजानोः पायुपर्यन्तमापां स्थानं प्रकीर्तितम् ।।८७।।
आपो ऽर्धचन्द्रं शुक्लं च वंबीजं परिकीर्तितम् ।
वारुणे वायुमारोप्य वकारेण समन्वितम् ।।८८।।
स्मरन्नारायणं देवं चतुर्बाहुं किरीटिनम् ।
शुद्धस्फटिकसंकाशं पीतवाससमच्युतम् ।।८९।।
धारयेत्पञ्च घटिकाः सर्वपापैः प्रमुच्यते ।
ततो जलाद्भयं नास्ति जले मृत्युर्न विद्यते ।।९०।।
ājānoḥ pāyuparyantamāpāṃ sthānaṃ prakīrtitam (87b)
āpo 'rdhacandraṃ śuklaṃ ca vaṃbījaṃ prakīrtitam
vāruṇe vāyumāropya vakāreṇa samanvitam (88)
smarannārāyaṇaṃ devaṃ caturbāhuṃ kirīṭinam
śuddhasphaṭikasaṃkāśaṃ pītavāsasamacyutam (89)
dhārayetpañca ghaṭikāḥ sarvapāpaiḥ pramucyate
tato jalādbhayaṃ nāsti jale mṛtyurna vidyate (90)

Anvay

sthānam: area; *ājānoḥ*: from the knees; *paryantam*: up to; *pāyu*: anus; *prakīrtitam*: is named; *āpaḥ*: water element; *śukla*: white; *ārdha*: half; *candram*: moon; *ca*: and; *bījam*: seed *mantra*, vibration; *prakīrtitam*: is called; *vam*: *vam*; *āropya*: directing; *vāyum*: breath; *vāruṇe*: within the region of *āpas*, water element; *samanvitam*: together with; *vakāreṇa*: sound *vam*; *smaran*: remembering; *catur-bāhum*: four-armed; *samacyutam*: imperishable; *devam*: god; *nārāyaṇa*: form of Viṣṇu; *kirīṭinam*: adorned with a crown; *saṃkāśam*: with the appearance; *śuddha*: pure; *sphaṭika*: crystal; *pīta*: orange; *vāsa*: garment; *dhārayet*: he should concentrate; *pañca ghaṭikāḥ*: two hours (5 x 24 minutes); *pramucyate*: he is freed; *sarva-pāpaiḥ*: from all sins; *tataḥ*: thus; *nāsti*: there is no; *bhayam*: fear; *jalāt*: of water; *mṛtyuḥ*: death; *na vidyate*: does not occur; *jale*: in water.

Translation

The area from the knees up to the anus is named *āpas*, water element. [The symbol is] a white half-moon and its *bīja mantra* is *vam*. Directing the breath within the region of the water element together with the sound *vam*, remembering the four-armed, imperishable god Nārāyaṇa, adorned with a crown, with the appearance of pure crystal, [and wearing] an orange garment, he should concentrate for two hours, [and then] he is freed from all sins. Thus there is no fear of water, [as his] death does not occur in water.

Commentary

These verses describe the method of *āpas dhāraṇā*, meditation on the water element. The location of the water element in the body is in-between the navel and the knees. The symbol of water is a white crescent moon. The moon is the symbol of water, because it relates with the tides and thus controls the seas. The color of āpas is white, which represents purity, as water washes all things clean. The seed sound vibration is *vam*, which is also the sound of the swādhiṣṭāna cakra, located in the region of the tailbone. As with the other elements, it should be remembered that the location of the water element in the body is different to that of the cakra.

In order to meditate on the water element, the practitioner should first direct the awareness into the region between the navel and the knees. Here the white crescent moon should be visualized. Rotate the awareness along the upper curve of the crescent moon from left to right, and then along the lower curve from right to left. See the white color. Feel the fluid quality and the coolness. Then rotate the breath together with the awareness, inhaling along the upper curve of the crescent moon from left to right, and then exhaling along the lower curve from right to left. Mentally intone the sound vibration *vam* together with the rotation of each breath.

When the concentration deepens and becomes spontaneous, begin to visualize the form of Nārāyaṇa, the imperishable lord, who sustains the universe. See Nārāyaṇa, lying in yoga nidrā, upon the serpent Ananta, floating on the ocean of milk. Nārāyaṇa has four arms and his form is transparent, like crystal, like clear water. He is wearing orange raiment, orange being the color of the swādhiṣṭāna lotus flower.

By meditating regularly in this way for a duration of two hours, the water element will be purified and strengthened. The practitioner will gradually become one with the water energy and will thus be freed from all sins and impurities. This yogi will have no fear of water. His or her death will not occur through water.

Verses 91, 92, 93 and 94a: Agni dhāraṇā

आपायोर्हृदयान्तं च वह्निस्थानं प्रकीर्तितम् ।
वह्निस्त्रिकोणं रक्तं च रेफाक्षरसमुद्भवम् ।।९१।।
वह्नौ चानिलमारोप्य रेफाक्षरसमुज्ज्वलम् ।
त्रियक्षं वरदं रुद्रं तरुणादित्यसंनिभम् ।।९२।।
भस्मोद्धूलितसर्वाङ्गं सुप्रसन्नमनुस्मरन् ।
धारयेत्पञ्च घटका वह्निनासौ न दह्यते ।।९३।।
न दह्यते शरीरं च प्रविष्टस्याग्निमण्डले ।९४।

āpāyorhṛdayāntaṃ ca vahnisthānaṃ prakīrtitam
vahnistrikoṇaṃ raktaṃ ca rephākṣarasamudbhavam (91)
vahnau cānilamāropya rephākṣarasamujjvalam
triyakṣaṃ varadaṃ rudraṃ taruṇādityasaṃnibham (92)
bhasmāddhūlitasarvāṅgaṃ suprasannamanusmaran
dhārayetpañca ghaṭikāḥ vahnināsau na dahyate (93)
na dahyate śarīraṃ ca praviṣṭasyāgnimaṇḍale (94a)

Anvay

āpāyoḥ: from water; *hṛdayāntam*: to the heart; *prakīrtitam*: is called; *sthānam*: site; *vahni*: of agni, fire element; *vahniḥ*: agni; *trikonam*: triangular in shape; *raktam*: red; *ca*: and; *samudbhavan*: is the source; *ākṣara*: letter of Sanskrit alphabet, subtle sound; *repha*: *ram*; *āropya*: directing; *vahnau*: within the fire element; *anilam*: vital air; *samujjvalam*: radiant; *dhārayet*: he should concentrate; *pañca ghaṭikāḥ*: two hours (5 x 24 minutes); *rudram*: *Rudra*; *smaran*: remembering; *suprasanna*: dazzling; *manu*: sovereign; *triyakṣam*: three eyes; *varadam*: grants boons; *samnibham*: resembles; *taruṇāditya*: newly risen sun; *ca*: and; *aṅgam*: limbs; *sarva*: all; *dhūlita*: bestrewn; *bhasmāt*: with ash; *asau*: that one; *na*: not; *dahyate*: burned; *vahninā*: by fire; *śarīram*: body; *ca praviṣṭasya*: even when it has entered; *agni-maṇḍale*: circle of fire, fire-pit.

Translation

From (the region of) water to the heart is called the site of *agni*, the fire element. (The symbol of) agni is a red triangle, and it is the source of the subtle sound *ram*. He should concentrate for two hours, directing the vital air, radiant with the mantra *ram,* within the fire element. Remembering Rudra, this dazzling sovereign, the three-eyed one, who grants boons, who resembles the newly risen sun, whose limbs are all smeared with ash, that one is not burned by fire. The body is not burned, even when it has entered the fire-pit.

Commentary

These verses describe the method of *agni dhāraṇā*, meditation on the fire element. The region of the water element is located from the knees to the navel. The location of the fire element is from the navel to the heart. The symbol of agni is a fiery red, inverted triangle, with the lower angle at the navel, and the upper two angles parallel with the heart. The fire element is the source of the bīja mantra *ram,* which is also the subtle sound associated with the maṇipura cakra, located behind the navel.

In order to meditate on the fire element, the practitioner should direct the awareness to this region between the navel and the heart. Visualize the radiant red, inverted triangle, filling this entire region with heat and light. Rotate the awareness along the three sides of the triangle, starting at the navel. Ascend along the right side, then cross over the top parallel to the heart, and descend along the left side. When this practice becomes familiar, add the rotation of the breath. Inhale up the right side, then hold the breath inside while moving across the top of the triangle, and exhale down the left side. When the rotation of the awareness and the breath become comfortable and continuous, add the repetition of the sound *ram* with each rotation.

This practice should continue until the awareness and the breath become subtle and deep, and the vision of the red inverted triangle becomes steady. Then begin to visualize the dazzling form of Rudra, the lord of fire. See the radiant red form of Rudra, which shines like the rising sun. Gaze at the three-eyed one, whose limbs are smeared with white ash. Feel the presence of Rudra, who easily grants boons to the supplicator.

By meditating in this way regularly for a period of two hours, the fire element is strengthened and purified. The body of that yogin has a radiant lustre, and is not burned by fire, even when he or she enters a fire-pit.

Verses 94b, 95, 96 and 97a: Vāyu dhāraṇā

आहृदयाद्भ्रूवोर्मध्यं वायुस्थानं प्रकीर्तितम् ।।९४।।
वायु: षत्कोणकं कृष्णं यकाराक्षरभासुरम् ।
मारुतं मरुतां स्थाने यकाराक्षरभासुरम् ।।९५।।
धारयेत्तत्र सर्वज्ञमीश्वरं विश्वतोमुखम् ।
धारयेत्पञ्च घटिका वायुवद्व्योमगो भवेत् ।।९६।।
मरणं न तु वायोश्च भयं भवति योगिन: ।९७।

āhṛdayādbhrūvormadhyaṃ vāyusthānaṃ prakīrtitam (94b)
vāyuḥ ṣaṭkoṇakaṃ kṛṣṇaṃ yakārākṣarabhāsuram
mārutaṃ marutāṃ sthāne yakārākṣarabhāsuram (95)
dhārayettatra sarvajñamīśvaraṃ viśvatomukham
dhārayetpañca ghaṭikā vāyuvadvyomago bhavet (96)
maraṇaṃ na tu vāyośca bhayaṃ bhavati yoginaḥ (97a)

Anvay

āhṛdayāt: from the heart; *bhrūvormadhyam*: to the eyebrow centre; *prakīrtitam*: is called; *sthānam*: site; *vāyuḥ*: of the air element; *ṣaṭkoṇakam*: hexagonal in shape; *kṛṣṇam*: blue; *bhāsuram*: glows with; *yakārākṣara*: sound vibration *yam*; *dhārayet*: he should concentrate on; *mārutam*: vital air; *bhāsuram*: radiating; *sthāne*: in the site of; *marutām*: Vayu; *tatra*: there; *dhārayet*: he should concentrate; *pañca ghaṭikā*: two hours; *sarvajñam*: all-knowing; *īśvaram*: Supreme Being; *mukham*: who has faces; *viśvataḥ*: on all sides; *vyomagaḥ*: siddhi of levitation; *bhavet*: comes into being; *vāyuvat*: through mastery of the air element; *bhayam*: fear; *vāyoḥ*: of air; *na bhavati*: cannot cause; *maraṇam*: death; *yoginaḥ*: of the yogin.

Translation

From the heart to the eyebrow centre is called the site of *vāyu*, the air element. [The symbol of] vāyu is hexagonal in shape, blue in color, and glows with the vibration *of yam*. He should concentrate for two hours on the vital air, radiating the vibration *yam,* at the site of vāyu, and then on the all-knowing Īśwara, the Supreme Being, who has faces on all sides. The siddhi of levitation arises through mastery of vāyu. Fear of wind [is overcome, because wind] cannot cause the death of the yogin.

Commentary

These verses describe the method of vāyu dhāraṇā, meditation on the air element. The region of the air element is in-between the heart and the eyebrow center. The symbol is a blue hexagon and the bīja mantra is *yam*, which is the same sound associated with the anāhata cakra, located behind the heart.

In order to perform this dhāraṇā, one should first bring the awareness into the region between the heart and the eyebrow center. Visualize the form of a large blue hexagon, filling this entire space. See one point of the hexagon at the heart, a second point at the eyebrow center, and two points to either side. Rotate the awareness around the six sides of the hexagon in a clockwise direction, seeing each side clearly. When the placement of the six sides of the hexagon is seen clearly, begin to rotate the breath along with the awareness, inhaling upward along the three sides to the right, and then exhaling downward along the three sides to the left. When this practice becomes comfortable, begin to mentally repeat the sound *yam, as* each side of the hexagon is traversed. With practice, it can be felt that the hexagon itself is radiating the sound *yam.*

When deep steadiness and stillness develop, and the awareness is totally merged in the practice, one should begin to visualize the all knowing Īśwara, the lord of air. Air flows everywhere, so Īśwara, the Supreme being, has faces on all sides. The yogi, who performs this practice regularly over a duration of time, develops the siddhi, or perfection, of levitation through the mastery of the air element. He or she becomes free from the fear of wind, because wind cannot be the cause of his or her death.

Verses 97b, 98, 99, 100, 101 and 102a: Ākāśa dhāraṇā

आभ्रूमध्यात्तु मूर्धान्तमाकाशस्थानमुच्यते ।।९७।।
व्योम वृत्तं च धूम्रं च हकाराश्चरभासुरम् ।
आकशे वायुमारोप्य हकारोपरि शंकरम् ।।९८।।
बिन्दुरूपं महादेवं व्योमाकारं सदाशिवम् ।
शुद्धस्फटिकसंकाशं धृतबालेन्दुमौलिनम् ।।९९।।
पञ्चवक्त्रयुतं सौम्यं दशबाहुं त्रिलोचनम् ।
सर्वायुधैर्धृताकरं सर्वभूषणभूषितम् ।।१००।।
उमार्धदेहं वरदं सर्वकारणकारणम् ।
आकाशधारणात्तस्य खेचरत्वं भवेद्ध्रुवम् ।।१०१।।
यत्रकुत्र स्थितो वापि सुखमत्यन्तमश्नुते ।१०२।
ābhrūmadhyāttu mūrdhāntamākāśasthānamucyate (97b)
vyoma vṛttaṃ ca dhūmraṃ ca hakārāścarabhāsuram
ākaśe vāyumāropya hakāropari śaṃkaram (98)
bindurūpaṃ mahādevaṃ vyomākāraṃ sadāśivam
śuddhasphaṭikasaṃkāśaṃ dhṛtabālendumaulinam (99)
pañcavaktrayutaṃ saumyaṃ daśabāhuṃ trilocanam
sarvāyudhairdhṛtākaraṃ sarvabhūṣaṇabhūṣitam (100)
umārdhadehaṃ varadaṃ sarvakāraṇakāraṇam
ākāśadhāraṇāttasya khecaratvaṃ bhaveddhruvam (101)
yatrakutra sthito vāpi sukhamatyantamaśnute (102a)

Anvay

tu: now; *ucyate*: it is said; *sthānam*: site; *ākāśa*: ether element; *ābhrūmadhyāt*: from the eyebrow centre; *mūrdhāntam*: to the crown of the head; *vyomaḥ*: ether element; *vṛttam*: circular; *ca*: and; *dhūmram*: smoky-grey; *bhāsuram*: glows with; *hakārāḥ-cara*: vibration *ham*; *āropya*: directing; *vāyum*: breath; *upari*: upwards; *ākāśe*: within the ether; *ha-kāra*: repeating *ham*; *dhāraṇāt*: he who concentrates; *mahādevam*: Supreme Deity; *sadāśiva*: manifestation of Śiva at the crown of the head, who is always auspicious; *śaṃkaram*: who is tranquil; *bindu-rūpam*: form of *bindu*, source of creation; *vyomākāram*: symbol of ether; *saṃkāśam*: shining like; *śuddha*: pure; *sphaṭika*: crystal; *dhṛta*: wearing; *bālendu*: crescent moon; *maulinam*: on his head; *yutam*: possessing; *pañca-vaktra*: five faces; *saumyam*: with pleasing expressions; *daśa-bāhum*: ten arms; *trilocanam*: three eyes; *dhṛtākaram*: armed with; *sarva-āyudhaiḥ*: all weapons; *bhūṣitam*: adorned with; *sarva-bhūṣaṇa*: all ornaments; *umā*: another name of Parvati, consort of Śiva; *ardha-deham*: half of his body; *varadam*: granting boons; *sarva-kāraṇa-kāraṇam*: cause of all causes; *tasya*: that [*yogin*]; *dhruvam*: certainly; *bhavet*: will be able; *khecaratvam*: to levitate; *vā-api*: and also; *aśnute*: enjoy; *atyantam*: endless; *sukham*: happiness; *yatrakutra*: wherever; *sthitaḥ*: he is.

Translation

Now, it is said, the site of *ākāśa* is from the eyebrow centre to the crown of the head. The (symbol of the) ether element is a smokey-grey circle, and it glows with the vibration *ham*. Directing the breath upwards within (the region of) ākāśa [he should] repeat the sound *ham.* (The deity of ākāśa is) Sadāśiva, who is tranquil, with the form of bindu, and the shape of vyoma. *(*He) shines like pure crystal, and is wearing a crescent moon on his head. (He) has five faces with pleasing expressions [and] three eyes. His ten arms hold all weapons [and are] adorned with all ornaments. Uma resides within half of his body, granting boons. That yogin who concentrates within ākāśa on the supreme deity, Sadāśiva, who is the cause of all causes, will certainly be able to levitate, and also enjoy endless happiness wherever he is.

Commentary

These verses describe the method of *ākāśa dhāraṇā*, meditation on the ether or space element. Ether, or space, is the subtlest element, and is also the vehicle of consciousness. The location of ākāśa in the physical body is between the eyebrow center and the crown of the head. The symbol for space is a circle, which has no beginning and no end. The color of the circle is said here to be smokey-grey. Other texts describe it as black, white or multi-colored. The color of the circle represents the void, which has no color, and yet contains the possibility of all colors. The circle of the void fills the space above the eyebrows, and it vibrates with the bija mantra *ham*.

The practitioner should direct his awareness into the space above the eyebrows, and visualize the circle of the void. Seeing the periphery of the circle clearly, he should rotate the awareness around it in a clockwise direction. When this rotation becomes effortless, he should add the awareness of the breath, so that each inhalation is one complete rotation of the circle and each exhalation is the next rotation. When this practice becomes spontaneous, the sound *ham* should be repeated together with each rotation of the breath. When the awareness becomes steady and one-pointed on the rotation of the breath and the sound around the perimeter of the circle, the practitioner should visualize the supreme deity, Sadāśiva, in the space of the circle.

Sadāśiva is calm and tranquil, and represents all auspiciousness. His form is also the *bindu*, or point of manifestation, indicating that he is the source of creation. He is the form of *vyoma,* or space, which is vast and unlimited, like the empty sky. He is transparent and shines like pure crystal. These are the symbols also found in the highest cakras. In ajña, there is the black *itarakya liṅgam*, or symbol of Śiva as the space of consciousness; in bindu the point of light in the space of consciousness, and in sahasrāra, the crystal lingam, the transparent form of Śiva, radiating the pure light of consciousness.

Sadāśiva wears the crescent moon on the crown of his head, which is another symbol of bindu cakra. The crescent moon represents the reflected wisdom of the pure consciousness, in the same way that the moon reflects the light of the sun. It is also the source of *amrit*, the eternal nectar, which drips down from bindu chakra into the body, conferring the energy of life, regeneration and transformation. Sadāśiva has five faces, each with three eyes and pleasing expressions. The five faces, which represent the five forms or aspects of Śiva, are as follows: (i) Īśāna, (ii) Tatpuruṣa, (iii) Aghora, (iv) Vamadeva, and (v) Sadyojaṭha.

These five faces of Śiva represent the five aspects of creation. The face of *Īśāna* is turned upward, and represents the highest aspect; it is also called Sadāśiva. This face represents the spiritual dimension, and is the deity which grants *mokṣa*, or liberation. It also represents the element of akasha. *Tatpuruṣa* faces east, rules over the air element and represents the forces of darkness and obscuration on the spiritual plane. *Aghora* faces south, and rules over the element of fire. It has the power of dissolution and regeneration. *Vamadeva* faces north, rules over the element water, and is responsible for preservation. *Sadyojaṭha* faces west, rules over the earth element, and represents the power of creation.

Each of these five faces has a pleasing expression, indicating their benign role in the process of creation and evolution. Each face is also described as having three eyes; two eyes which see the external existence and the third eye in the middle, which sees the subtle existence within. Sadāśiva, comprising the five aspects or faces of creation, is said to have ten arms, each holding different weapons. The five hands on the right side display a trident, axe, sword, bow, and *abhaya mudra*, gesture of fearlessness or protection. The five hands on the left side display a noose, snake, bell, sheath of arrows and *varada mudrā*, gesture of compassion or bestowing of boons.

The ten arms of Sadāśiva are also adorned with beautiful gems and ornaments. These two aspects, the weapons and the ornaments, represent the power of Sadāśiva to protect the creation, and also to provide it with the essence of beauty and value. He is also known as *Ardhanareśwara*, the androgenous Śiva, because Uma, his consort, who represents the cosmic energy, resides within the left half of his body, bestowing boons upon the creation. The verse further states, that yogin, who concentrates within the region of ākāśa, between the eyebrows and the crown of the head, on the supreme deity, Sadāśiva, who is the cause of all causes, will certainly be able to levitate, and will enjoy endless happiness wherever he may be.

Verses 102b and 103: Means to attain immortality

एवं च धारणा: पञ्च कुर्याद्योगी विचक्षण: ।।१०२।।
ततो दृढशरीर: स्यान्मृत्युस्तस्य न विद्यते ।
ब्रह्मण: प्रलयेनापि न सीदति महामति: ।।१०३।।
evaṃ ca dhāraṇāḥ pañca kuryādyogī vicakṣaṇaḥ (102b)
tato dṛḍhaśarīraḥ syānmṛtyustasya na vidyate
brahmaṇaḥ pralayenāpi na sīdati mahāmatiḥ (103)

Anvay

ca: and; *evam*: so; *vicakṣaṇaḥ*: accomplished; *yogī*: *yogin*; *kuryāt*: should perform; *pañca*: five; *dhāraṇāḥ*: types of concentration; *tataḥ*: then; *śarīraḥ*: body; *syāt*: becomes; *dṛḍha*: strong; *mṛtyuḥ*: death; *na*: not; *vidyate*: is known; *tasya*: to him; *mahāmatiḥ*: wise man; *na*: not; *sīdati*: does perish; *api*: even; *pralayena*: dissolution of the manifest cosmos into the unmanifest; *brahmanaḥ*: of Brahma, all-pervading creator.

Translation

And so the accomplished yogin should perform [these] five dhāraṇās. Then his body becomes strong [and] death is not known to him. The wise man does not perish, even at the time of *pralaya*, when the universe is dissolved back into Brahma.

Commentary

The physical body is comprised of the five elements. The proficient yogi should practise these five dhāraṇās because, by doing so, the five elements are purified, rebalanced and regenerated. When the elements are regenerated, the body becomes strong and immutable. In ordinary persons, disease, ageing and death are due to the imbalance and weakening of the elements, which is the natural cause of degeneration. For example, when the earth element weakens, the bones and nails become brittle, the muscles flacid, and the teeth and hair fall out. When the water element weakens, the body withers and the hair goes grey. When the fire element weakens, the skin becomes dull, and the digestion and metabolism are slowed. When the air element weakens, the nerves are affected and palsy sets in. When the ether element weakens, the mind is affected and the memory is impaired.

By the practice of these five dhāraṇās, the elemental forces become immutable. The body of that yogi, who masters the elemental forces, does not weaken, age or perish. Death cannot come to him or her unbidden, even at the time of universal dissolution, when the entire manifest existence is reabsorbed back into the unmanifest by Brahma, the lord of creation.

Verses 104, 105 and 106: Dhyāna

समभ्यसेत्तथा ध्यानं घटकाषष्टिमेव च ।
वायुं निरुध्य चाकाशे देवतामिष्टदामिति ।।१०४।।
सगुणं ध्यानमेतत्स्यादणिमादिगुणप्रदम् ।
निर्गुणध्यानयुक्तस्य समाधिश्च ततो भवेत् ।।१०५।।
दिनद्वादशकेनैव समाधि समवाप्नुयात्
वायुं निरुध्य मेधावि जीवन्मुक्तो भवत्ययम् ।।१०६।।
samabhyasettathā dhyānaṃ ghaṭikāṣaṣṭimeva ca
vāyuṃ nirudhya cākāśe devatāmiṣṭadāmiti (104)
saguṇaṃ dhyānametatsyādaṇimādiguṇapradam
nirguṇadhyānayuktasya samādhiśca tato bhavet (105)
dinadvādaśakenaiva samādhi samavāpnuyāt
vāyuṃ nirudhya medhāvī jīvanmukto bhavatyayam (106)

Anvay
tathā: then; *nirudhya*: holding; *vāyum*: breath; *ṣaṣṭim*: six; *ākāśe*: in the ether element; *samabhyaset*: he should practise; *ghaṭikā*: period of twenty four minutes; *dhyānam*: deep meditation; *devatām*: on the deity; *dām*: grants; *iṣṭa*: wishes; *iti*: it is said; *etat*: this; *syāt*: is; *saguna dhyāna*: meditation on the deity with form and qualities; *pradam*: which bestows; *guṇa*: attributes; *ādi*: beginning with; *aṇimā*: power of making the body small and subtle; *ca*: and; *tataḥ*: thus; *yuktasya*: he is merged in; *nirguṇa-dhyāna*: meditation on the deity without form and qualities; *bhavet*: attains; *samādhiḥ*: state of unity with the deity; *samavāpnuyāt*: he should obtain; *eva*: just; *dvādaśakena*: within twelve; *dina*: days; *nirudhya*: having retained; *vāyum*: breath; *ayam*: this; *medhāvi*: wise one; *bhavati*: becomes; *jīvanmuktaḥ*: liberated while living in the body.

Translation
Then, holding the breath in the ether element, he should practise deep meditation on the deity with form and qualities,

who grants his wishes, for six *ghaṭikas* (two hours and twenty four minutes). It is said this is *saguna dhyāna*, meditation on form, which bestows attributes, beginning with anima, the power of making the body small and subtle. And thus he is merged in *nirguna dhyāna*, formless meditation, and attains *samādhi,* transcendental meditation. He should obtain this within just twelve days. Having retained the breath, this wise one becomes a *jīvanmukta,* liberated while still living in the body.

Commentary

These verses describe the attainment of the higher stages of meditation, *dhyāna* and *samādhi*, as it was experienced by the yogis of old. Holding the breath can be understood as breath retention in conjunction with the practice of pranayama. However, here it refers to focusing the breath and breathing into the region of ākāśa for a period of about two and a half hours. This is the period considered to be necessary for a practitioner to enter into a deep state of meditation. The space of ākāśa, as described earlier, can be experienced between the eyebrows and the crown of the head. While breathing in and out of this space, one should concentrate on the personal form of one's deity, who grants all wishes.

Space is the substratum for all manifestation, and therefore, everything exists within it. The deity visualized in the space represents the subtle source of all existence, and is therefore the one, who grants all wishes. The practitioner should imagine or visualize the deity in the illumined space of consciousness, which is within everything, and at the same time, beyond everything. This pure consciousness can assume or manifest all forms, but in itself is formless. This practice of meditation is called *saguṇa dhyāna*, deep meditation on form, which bestows certain attributes, or siddhis, when it is perfected. The first of these powers is referred to here as *aṇima*, the ability of subtlety, by which physical mass and density can be reduced at will.

When saguṇa dhyāna is perfected, one merges into the state of *nirguṇa dhyāna*, deep formless meditation, and thus attains samādhi, the transcendental state. The verse further states that the yogi should attain this state within twelve days, providing the practice is performed correctly. Hence, having focused the breath and the mind in deep meditation within the region of space, the wise person becomes a *jīvanmukta*, liberated while living in the body.

Verses 107 and 108: Samādhi

समाधिः समतावस्था जीवात्मपरमात्मनोः ।
यदि स्वदेहमुत्स्रष्टुमिच्छा चेदुत्सृजेत्स्वयम् ।।१०७।।
परब्रह्मणि लीयेत न तस्योत्क्रान्तिरिष्यते ।
अथ नो चेत्समुत्स्रष्टुं स्वशरीरं प्रियं यदि ।।१०८।।
samādhiḥ samatāvasthā jīvātmaparamātmanoḥ
yadi svadehamutsrastumicchā cedutsrjetsvayam (107)
parabrahmaṇi līyeta na tasyotkrāntiriṣyate
atha no cetsamutsrastuṃ svaśarīraṃ priyaṃ yadi (108)

Anvay
samādhiḥ: unity with highest consciousness; *avasthā*: state; *jīvātma*: individual self; *paramātmanoḥ*: and the cosmic self; *samatā*: same; *yadi*: if; *icchā*: desire; *utsraṣṭum*: to abandon; *sva*: his own; *deham*: body; *utsṛjet*: can be accomplished; *svayam*: by himself; *līyeta*: attached; *parabrahmani*: to the supreme reality; *tasya*: he; *na iṣyate*: does not seek; *utkrāntiḥ*: to ascend.

Translation
Samādhi is the state [in which] the individual soul and the cosmic soul [are] the same. If (the yogin) desires to abandon the body, this can be accomplished by himself. Being attached to the supreme reality, he does not seek to ascend.

Commentary
In these verses, *samādhi* is described as the state of union between the *ātman* and the *paramātman*. The atman, or self, is the individual field of consciousness. The paramātman, or supreme self, is the cosmic field of consciousness. When the spirit is born in the body, the unlimited, or supreme, consciousness becomes limited to that particular individual being. The consciousness, being limited, is then perceived by the individual as comprising different states of consciousness

such as: conscious, subconscious, and unconscious. In the state of samādhi, this limitation or division of consciousness is transcended. The individual consciousness merges into the cosmic consciousness.

In samādhi, the embodied state of existence is transcended, although there is still a connection between the body and the consciousness. Usually, the yogin will return to the body via this connection and resume his or her physical existence. It is said that the consciousness may remain outside of the body in this way for a period of up to thirteen days. If the yogin wishes to remain in the super-conscious state beyond this period, the connection between the body and the consciousness will be severed, so that returning to the body will no longer be possible. Similarly, if the yogin should wish to abandon the body, this can also be accomplished at the time of his or her choosing, by entering the state of samādhi with the intention of not returning to the physical body.

Swami Satyananda, a great yogin of the 20th century, chose to leave his body in this way. On December 5th, 2009, he informed his disciple, Swami Satyasangananda, that he would leave his body that evening. He said that he had chosen that particular date and time, as it offered the best possible window for his ascension. At 8:00 pm, he sat down in his room in the company of his disciple and entered the state of samādhi. Over the next few hours, his disciple was able to witness the process of his ascension, as the prāṇas and consciousness of the master gradually rose upward and departed from the opening at the top back of the head. Around midnight, the doctor was called in, and after examining the body, he declared that Swami Satyananda had passed on.

An accomplished yogin is able to leave the body at will, because he has transcended the physical identity and all the desires that it ignites. Even while living in the body, during the course of his life and practice, the yogin has entered the supreme consciousness many times and become familiar with this transcendental state of being. In this way, he detaches himself from the physical state, and slowly attaches himself to *parabrahman*, the supreme state of ever-expanding consciousness. When this shift in consciousness is made, the yogin no longer seeks to ascend; he has ascended. The desire to ascend indicates that the transition from individual identity to cosmic consciousness is not yet complete.

Verses 109, 110 and 111: Liberation

सर्वलोकेषु विहरन्नणिमादिगुणान्वितः ।
कदाचित्स्वेच्छया देवो भूत्वा स्वर्गे महीयते ।।१०९।।
मनुष्यो वापि यक्षो वा स्वेच्छयापीक्षणाद्भवेत् ।
सिंहो व्याघ्रो गजो वाश्वः स्वेच्छया हुतामियात् ।।११०।।
यथेष्टमेव वर्तेत यद्वा योगी महेश्वरः ।
अभ्यासभेदतो भेदः फलं तु सममेव हि ।।१११।।
sarvalokeṣu viharannaṇimādiguṇānvitaḥ
kadācitsvecchayā devo bhūtvā svarge mahīyate (109)
manuṣyo vāpi yakṣo vā svecchayāpīkṣaṇādbhavet
siṃho vyāghro gajo vāśvaḥ svecchayā bahutāmiyāt (110)
yatheṣṭameva varteta yadvā yogī maheśvaraḥ
abhyāsabhedato bhedaḥ phalaṃ tu samameva hi (111)

Anvay
anvitaḥ: endowed with; *guṇa*: attributes; *ādi*: such as; *aṇimā*: power of making the body small and subtle; *viharan*: he moves; *sarva-lokeṣu*: within all the worlds; *kadācit*: at times; *bhūtvā*: having become; *devaḥ*: divine being; *svecchayā*: through his own will; *mahīyate*: he is highly honoured; *svarge*: in the celestial world; *vā*: or; *api*: even; *bhavet*: he may take on; *svecchayā*: through his own will; *īkṣaṇāt*: appearance; *manuṣyaḥ*: man; *yakṣaḥ*: demi-god; *iyāt*: he may go; *svecchayā*: by his own will; *bahutām*: in many forms; *siṃhaḥ*: lion; *vyāghraḥ*: tiger; *gajaḥ*: elephant; *vā*: or; *aśvaḥ*: horse; *yogī*: *yogin*; *yadvā*: who is like; *maheśvaraḥ*: Supreme Lord; *varteta*: exists; *yathā*: in accordance with; *eva*: his own; *iṣṭam*: wishes; *bhedaḥ*: difference; *bhedataḥ*: various; *abhyāsa*: practices; *tu . . . eva hi*: but . . . indeed; *phalam*: result; *samam*: same.

Translation
Endowed with attributes, such as *aṇima,* the power of making the body minute and subtle, he moves within all the

worlds. At times, having become a *deva,* divine being, through his own will, he is highly honoured in the celestial world. Or, through his own will, he may even take the appearance of a man or a *yakṣa,* demi-god. By his own will, he may move in many forms, [such as] a lion, tiger, elephant or horse. The *yogin,* who is like the supreme lord, exists in accordance with his own wishes. [There is] a difference in the various practices, but indeed the result is the same.

Commentary

These verses describe the life of the accomplished yogin. Being endowed with all the *siddhis*, or attributes of perfection, such as *aṇima*, the power of making the body subtle and imperceptible, he moves freely within all the worlds, or planes of existence. At times, by the power of his own will, he transforms himself into a *deva*, luminous divine being, and is highly honored in the heavenly realms. At other times, again by the power of his own will, he may assume the appearance of a man or a demi-god. He is also able to move about in many animal forms by his own will, such as a lion, tiger, elephant or horse. This yogin, being liberated from a particular identity and merged with the totality of consciousness, is like the supreme lord, and exists in accordance with his own wishes. Finally, the verse says, there are many different yogic practices, which one may choose to perfect, but the result of them all is the same—liberation.

Verses 112, 113, 114 and 115a: Mahābandha

पार्ष्णिं वामस्य पादस्य योनिस्थाने नियोजयेत् ।
प्रसार्य दक्षिणं पादं हस्ताभ्यां धारयेद्दृढम् ।।११२।।
चुबुकं हृदि विन्यस्य पूरयेद्वायुना पुनः ।
कुम्भकेन यथाशक्ति धारयित्वा तु रेचयेत् ।।११३।।
वामाङ्गेन समभ्यस्य दक्षाङ्गेन ततो ऽभ्यसेत् ।
प्रसारितस्तु यः पादस्तमूरूपरि नामयेत् ।।११४।।
अयमेव महाबन्ध उभयत्रैवमभ्यसेत् ।११५।
pārṣṇiṃ vāmasya pādasya yonisthāne niyojayet
prasārya dakṣiṇaṃ pādaṃ hastābhyāṃ dhārayeddṛḍham(112)
cubukaṃ hṛdi vinyasya pūrayedvāyunā punaḥ
kumbhakena yathāśakti dhārayitvā tu recayet (113)
vāmāṅgena samabhyasya dakṣāṅgena tato 'bhyaset
prasāritastu yaḥ pādastamūrūpari nāmayet (114)
ayameva mahābandha ubhayatraivamabhyaset (115a)

Anvay

niyojayet: he should press; *pārṣṇim*: heel; *vāmasya pādasya*: of the left foot; *sthāne*: within the region; *yoni*: perineum; *prasārya*: having extended; *dakṣiṇam pādam*: right leg; *dhārayet*: he should hold; *dṛḍham*: firmly; *hastābhyām*: with both hands; *vinyasya*: placing; *cubukam*: chin; *hṛdi*: on the chest; *pūrayet-vāyunā*: he should inhale; *punaḥ*: again; *dhārayitvā*: maintaining; *kumbhakena*: breath retention; *yathāśakti*: as long as possible; *tu*: then; *recayet*: he should exhale; *samabhyasya*: having practised; *vāma-aṅgena*: with the left foot; *tataḥ*: then; *abhyaset*: he should practise; *dakṣa-aṅgena*: with the right foot; *nāmayet*: he should bend; *yaḥ*: whichever; *pādaḥ*: leg; *prasāritaḥ*: is stretched out; *pari*: against; *ūrū*: thigh; *ayam-eva*: this is; *mahābandha*: *mahābandha*, great lock; *evam*: in this way; *abhyaset*: it should be practised; *ubhayatra*: on both sides.

Translation
He should press the heel of the left foot in the region of the perineum. Having extended the right leg, he should hold [it] firmly with both hands. Placing the chin on the chest, he should inhale again. Maintaining breath retention for as long as possible, he should then exhale. Having practised with the left foot, he should then practise with the right. He should then bend whichever leg is stretched out against the thigh. This is *mahābandha*; in this way it should be practised on both sides.

Commentary
Here the practice of mahābandha is described. Mahābandha, the great lock, is a higher practice of haṭha yoga, which is used to awaken the kuṇḍalinī, and free it from obstruction at the level of the mūlādhāra and viśuddhi cakras.

The instruction begins with the description of *uttanpadāsana.* Sitting with both legs outstretched in front, one should bend the left knee, and press the left heel into the region of the perineum. Next, keeping the right leg outstretched, one should grasp the toes of the right foot with both hands and hold them firmly. While holding this position, inhale deeply and bend the head forward, placing the chin on the chest. Inhale again a little more with the head down, and then retain the breath inside for as long as possible. At the end of the breath retention, raise the head and then slowly exhale.

After completing the round of practice with the left foot pressed into the perineum, one should change legs and practice with the left leg extended and the right foot pressed into the perineum.

In this way, the technique should be practised on both sides.

At the completion of the practice, one should bend the outstretched leg, so that the sole of that foot presses against the opposite thigh, as in the meditation āsana, called siddhāsana. This is mahābandha.

In other haṭha yoga texts, mahābandha incorporates all three of the bandhas: mūla bandha, uḍḍiyāna bandha and jālandhara bandha. Mūlabandha is the perineal lock, which was described in the technique above, by pressing the heel into the perineum, and pulling upward on the muscles in this region. Jālandhara bandha is the chin lock, described as bending the head forward until the chin touches the chest. However, uḍḍiyāna bandha, the abdominal lock, is not included in the above practice.

Mahābandha is traditionally performed in the cross-legged meditation posture, called siddhāsana; whereas the practice described here is performed in uttānpādāsana, with one leg stretched forward and the other leg bent. Therefore, we would say that the above description could also be an early version of the practice of mahāvedha mudrā.

Verses 115b, 116 and 117a: Mahāvedha mudrā

वायुनां गतिमावृत्य निभृतं कण्ठमुद्रया ।
पुटद्वयं समाक्रम्य वामहाबन्धस्थितो योगी कृत्वा पूरकमेकधी: ।।११५।।
यु: स्फुरति सत्वरम् ।।११६।।
अयमेव महावेध: सिद्धैरभ्यस्यते ऽनिशम् ।११७।
mahābandhasthito yogī kṛtvā pūrakamekadhīḥ (115b)
vāyunāṃ gatimāvṛtya nibhṛtaṃ kaṇṭhamudrayā
puṭadvayaṃ samākramya vāyuḥ sphurati satvaram (116)
ayameva mahāvedhaḥ siddhairabhyasyate 'niśam (117a)

Anvay

yogī: yogin; *sthitaḥ*: in the position of; *mahābandha*: great lock; *kṛtvā pūrakam*: having inhaled; *ekadhīḥ*: his mind still; *āvṛtya nibhṛtam*: stops; *kaṇṭha-mudrayā*: by means of the throat lock; *gatim*: flow; *vāyunām*: of the prāṇas, five vital energies; *samākramya*: having entered; *puṭa-dvayam*: two-sided cavity, two nāḍīs, iḍā and piṅgalā; *vāyuḥ*: prāṇa; *sphurati*: vibrates; *satvaram*: quickly; *ayam-eva*: this is; *mahāvedhaḥ*: great piercer; *abhyasyate*: it is practised; *aniśam*: continually; *siddhaiḥ*: by accomplished yogins who have obtained the eight supernatural powers.

Translation

The *yogin*, (sitting) in the position of mahābandha, having inhaled, with his mind still, stops the flow of the prāṇas by means of the throat lock. The two nāḍīs, iḍā and piṅgalā, having entered (suṣumnā), the prāṇa vibrates quickly. This is *mahāvedha*; it is practised continually by the siddhas.

Commentary

Here the practice of mahāvedha mudrā is described. This is an earlier rendition of the technique, which later developed as a mudrā of haṭha yoga, and also of kriyā yoga. The root *mahā* means 'great', *vedha* means 'piercing' and *mudrā* means ‘attitude’. So this is the great piercing attitude or movement, which causes the kuṇḍalinī śakti to pierce through the opening of suṣumnā and rise upward to the brain.

The yogin should sit in the position of mahābandha, described above. Next he should inhale deeply, hold the breath inside, and bend the head forward into the throat lock. Retaining the breath inside for as long as possible in this position, the mind becomes very still and the flow of prāṇa is stopped by means of the throat lock.

When the activity of the mind and prāṇa cease, the two nāḍīs, iḍā and piṅgalā, become balanced and merge with suṣumnā. This causes the prāṇa to vibrate at a higher velocity, forcing the kuṇḍalinī śakti to pierce the suṣumnā and rise upward to the higher centers.

This method of mahāvedha is practised by the accomplished yogins, who wish to awaken the kuṇḍalinī, and maintain this awakening during their lifetime.

Verses 117b and 118a: Khecarī mudrā

अन्तःकपालकुहरे जिह्वां व्यावृत्य धारयेत् ।।११७।।
भ्रूमध्यदृष्टिरप्येषा मुद्रा भवति खेचरी ।११८।
antaḥkapālakuhare jihvāṃ vyāvṛtya dhārayet (117b)
bhrūmadhyadṛṣṭirapyeṣā mudrā bhavati khecarī (118a)

Anvay
vyāvṛtya: folding back; *jihvām*: tongue; *kuhare*: within the cavity; *antaḥ*: inside; *kapāla*: head; *dhārayet*: he should fix; *dṛṣṭiḥ*: gaze; *bhrūmadhya*: on the point between the eyebrows; *api*: then; *eṣā*: this; *bhavati*: is; *khecarī mudrā*: tongue lock.

Translation
Folding the tongue back within the cavity inside the head, he should fix the gaze on the point between the eyebrows; then this is *khecarī mudrā.*

Commentary
Khecarī mudrā is an ancient practice, found in the yoga upaniṣads and in all the classical texts on haṭha yoga. Although it is regarded as a physical practice today, the yogis of old used it as a complete form of meditation in itself in order to attain the transcendental state of consciousness. The root *khe* comes from the word *kha,* meaning 'sky', and *cari* or *carya* means 'to roam'. When the practice of khecarī mudrā is perfected and performed regularly for long periods, it allows the yogin to roam freely in the vast sky, or space, of the higher consciousness. The technique given here is as follows:

Sitting in a comfortable and steady meditation āsana, one should close the eyes and allow the body and mind to become still. Next, fold the tongue back as far as possible into the cavity at the back of the throat. Maintaining this position for as long as possible, one should focus the awareness and the inner gaze upon the point of ajña cakra, in-between the eyebrows. At first, it may be necessary to release the tongue frequently, relax it and then resume the mudrā. With practice, however, it becomes easier to maintain the position for longer periods of time.

This is khecarī mudrā, the attitude of dwelling in the highest consciousness.

Verses 118b and 119a: Jālandhara bandha

कण्ठमाकुञ्चय हृदये स्थापयेद्दृढया धिया ।।११८।।
बन्धो जालंधराख्यो ऽयं मृत्युमातङ्ककेसरी ।११९।
kaṇṭhamākuñcaya hṛdaye sthāpayeddṛḍhayā dhiyā (118b)
bandho jālaṃdharākhyo 'yaṃ mṛtyumātaṅkakesarī (119a)

Anvay
ākuñcaya: contracting; *kaṇṭham*: throat; *sthāpayet*: he should place; *dṛḍhayā dhiyā*: with focused mind; *hṛdaye*: on the chest; *ayam*: this; *ākhyaḥ*: is called; *jālaṃdhara bandhaḥ*: throat lock; *kesarī*: lion; *ātaṅka*: to the fear; *mṛtyum*: of death.

Translation
Contracting the throat, he should place [the chin] on the chest with focused mind. This is called jālandhara bandha [and] is a lion to the fear of death.

Commentary
Jālandhara is one of the four bandhas, or psychic locks. It is performed by bending the head forward, so that the chin touches the chest. In this pose, the awareness should be focused on the point where the chin meets the chest. Bending the head forward in this manner contracts the region of viśuddhi cakra, which is located behind the throat pit.

The word jālandhara is comprised of two roots: *jāla* means 'net', and *dhara* is a 'flow'. According to the philosophy of Tantra, the *amṛta*, or nectar of life, flows down through the body from bindu cakra, which is located at the top back of the head. This nectar contains two properties: amṛta, immortal life, and *viś,* poison, that is responsible for degeneration, disease, old age and death. As long as the nectar remains within the higher consciousness, in the region of the head, the viś aspect does not become active. However, when the nectar flows downward into the body, the viś is activated.

The purpose of viśuddhi cakra is to purify, or process, the nectar before it flows down into the body in order to remove the vish. The words viś and *śuddhi,* 'purification' are contained within the term viśuddhi. However, viśuddhi can only process the nectar (i) if this center is activated, and (ii) if the nectar is held within this center for a duration of time. Jālandhara acts as a net at the base of the neck for catching the flow of nectar, before it drips down into the body, along with the property of viś, or poison, which causes degeneration.

The regular practice of jālandhara bandha activates viśuddhi cakra, and enables it to become a processing center for the flow of amṛta. When the degenerative properties are removed from the amṛta on an ongoing basis, the body of the yogin is said to become free from aging, disease and death. Hence, this verse describes jālandhara bandha as a lion to the fear of death. Just as the lion roams the jungle fearlessly, the yogin who perfects the practice of jālandhara bandha, lives in this world free from the fear of degeneration, disease and death.

Verses 119b and 120a: Uḍḍiyāna bandha

बन्धो येन सुषुम्नायां प्राणस्तूड्डीयते यतः ।।११९।।
उड्ड्यानाख्यो हि बन्धो ऽयं योगिभिः समुदाहृतः ।१२०।
bandho yena suṣumnāyāṃ prāṇastūḍḍīyate yataḥ (119b)
uḍḍyānākhyo hi bandho 'yaṃ yogibhiḥ samudāhṛtaḥ (120a)

Anvay

tu: now; *yataḥ*: that; *bandhaḥ*: lock; *yena*: by which; *prāṇa*: vital energy; *uḍḍīyate*: flies up; *suṣumnāyām*: through suṣumnā, central energy channel in the spine; *samudāhṛtaḥ*: is called; *uḍḍīyāna bandhaḥ*: abdominal lock; *yogibhiḥ*: by the yogins.

Translation

Now that bandha by which the prāṇa flies upward through suṣumnā is called *uḍḍīyāna bandha* by the yogins.

Commentary

If the amṛta, or nectar of life, that falls down from bindu cakra, is not filtered in the net of jālandhara bandha and processed at viśuddhi cakra, then it falls down into the body and collects at maṇipura cakra, behind the navel. Here it maintains the life force, but also its antithesis, the force of degeneration, disease and death.

Uḍḍīyāna bandha is known as the abdominal lock. It is performed by drawing the abdomen inward and then upward, causing an upsurge of energy. The word *uḍḍīyāna* means 'to rise up', 'to fly up'. Uḍḍīyāna bandha is the psychic lock, which causes the prāṇa, or the amṛta, that is collected and stored at the maṇipura cakra to fly upward through the suṣumnā nāḍī to the brain and the higher centers of consciousness.

Verses 120b and 121a: Yoni or mūla bandha

पार्ष्णिभागेन सम्पीड्य योनिमाकुञ्चयेद्दृढम् ।।१२०।।
अपानमूर्ध्वमुत्थाप्य योनिबन्धो ऽयमुच्यते ।१२१।
pārṣṇibhāgena saṃpīḍya yonimākuñcayeddṛḍham (120b)
apānamūrdhvamutthāpya yonibandho 'yamucyate (121a)

Anvay
ākuñcayet: he should contract; *dṛḍham*: firmly; *yonim*: perineum; *saṃpīḍya*: by means of pressure; *bhāgena*: with part; *pārṣṇi*: of the heel; *utthāpya*: raising; *apānam*: vital energy which moves downward from navel to perineum; *ūrdhvam*: upwards; *ayam*: this; *ucyate*: is called; *yonibandhaḥ*: perineum lock.

Translation
He should firmly contract the perineum by means of pressure with part of the heel, raising the *apāna* upwards; this is called *yoni bandha.*

Commentary
This verse describes the practice of yoni bandha, also called mūla bandha, contraction of the perineum. Yoni or mūla bandha activates the mūlādhāra cakra, which is located below the tip of the spinal column, two centimeters interior to the perineum in the male body, and at the outer surface of the cervix in the female body.

Applying pressure to the perineum with the heel, suggests that the practitioner would sit in *siddhāsana*, or *siddhayoni āsana*, with the sole of the right foot placed flat against the inner left thigh and the right heel pressing firmly against the perineum. The toes of the left foot are wedged into the space between the right calf and thigh. The left heel rests on top of the right heel, exerting a mild pressure against the pubic bone, which is the triggerpoint for swādhiṣṭhāna cakra.

Apāna is one of the five flows of prānic energy, which sustain the physical body from within. Apāna flows downward in the pelvic region from the waist to the pelvic floor, and is responsible for the processes of evacuation in this area. By the practice of mūlabandha, this downward flow of prāṇa is reversed, and directed upward to ajña cakra, at the mid-brain. This is very beneficial for meditation, and for activating the mental processes. It helps to raise the energies, thereby removing negative states, such as anxiety, depression and mental dissipation.

Verses 121b, 122, 123 and 124a: Viparīta karaṇī mudrā with mūlabandha

प्राणापानौ नादबिन्दू मूलबन्धेन चैकताम् ।।१२१।।
गत्वा योगस्य संसिद्धिं यच्छतो नात्र संशयः ।
करणी विपरीताख्या सर्वव्याधिविनाशिनी ।।१२२।।
नित्यमभ्यासयुक्तस्य जाठराग्निविवर्धनी ।
आहारो बहुलस्तस्य संपाद्यः साधकस्य च ।।१२३।।
अल्पाहारो यदि भवेदग्निर्देहं हरेत्क्षणात् ।१२४।
prāṇāpānau nādabindu mūlabandhena caikatām (121b)
gatvā yogasya saṃsiddhiṃ yacchato nātra saṃśayaḥ
karaṇī viparītākhyā sarvavyādhivināśinī (122)
nityamabhyāsayuktasya jāṭharāgnivivardhanī
āhāro bahulastasya saṃpadyaḥ sādhakasya ca (123)
alpāhāro yadi bhavedagnirdehaṃ haretkṣaṇāt (124a)

Anvay

prāṇa-apāna: prāṇa-apāna; *ca*: and; *nāda-bindu*: nāda (subtle sound vibration) and bindu (point of origin); *ekatām*: are united; *mūlabandhena*: through mūlabandha, perineal lock; *gatvā*: attaining; *saṃsiddhim*: success; *yogasya*: in *yoga*; *yacchataḥ*: there is; *na*; no; *saṃśayaḥ*: doubt; *atra*: here; *karaṇī*: performing; *viparīta*: inverted; *yuktasya*: by one engaged in; *nityam*: continual; *abhyāsa*: practice; *ākhyā*: is said; *vivardhanī*: to increase; *jāṭhara-agni*: digestive fire; *vināśinī*: removing; *sarva*: all; *vyādhi*: diseases; *bahulastasya*: abundance [of food]; *āhāraḥ*: should be brought; *ca*: and; *saṃpadyaḥ*: consumed; *sādhakasya*: by the aspirant; *yadi*: if; *alpa*: little; *bhavet*: is; *āhāraḥ*: supplied; *agniḥ*: fire; *kṣaṇāt*: immediately; *haret*: will take; *deham*: body.

Translation

Prāṇa/apāna and *nāda/bindu*, are united through (the practice of) mūlabandha (combined with) viparīta karaṇī (mudrā). Success in yoga is attained by one who engages in this practice regularly; there is no doubt here. This practice is said to increase the digestive fire, removing all diseases. An abundance of food should be brought and consumed by the aspirant. If little is supplied, the fire will immediately take his body.

Commentary

Viparīta karaṇī mudrā is the inverted āsana, performed in the lying position, with the legs raised, so that the feet are above the head and the back is at a 45 degree angle with the floor. When mūlabandha is performed in this posture, the downward flow of apāna is easily reversed and united with prana, the energy which flows upward in the region of the chest, from the diaphragm to the shoulders.

On account of the inverted posture, the combined energies of prāṇa and apāna flow naturally into the neck and head region, activating the bindu cakra, at the top back of the head. Bindu cakra is the center of nāda, the cosmic sound, and bindu, the cosmic point of origin. The union of nāda and bindu result in transcendence, and hence success in yoga is attained by one, who performs this practice regularly.

Due to the inverted posture and the reversal of the prāṇas, this practice also activates the energy of samāna, located in the region between the waist and the diaphragm. This increases the digestive fire and removes all diseases, which are associated with low energy in this area. When the digestive fire is enhanced, however, one must take care to consume adequate food. If too little food is taken, the digestive fire will deplete the body.

Verses 124b, 125, 126a: Method of rejuvenation

अधःशिरश्चोर्ध्वपादः क्षणं स्यात्प्रथमे दिने ।।१२४।।
क्षणात्तु किंचिदधिकमभ्यसेत्तु दिनेदिने ।
वली च पलितं चैव षण्मासार्धान्न दृश्यते ।।१२५।।
याममात्रं तु यो नित्यमभ्यसेत्स तु कालजित् ।१२६।
adhaḥśiraścordhvapādaḥ kṣaṇaṃ syātprathame dine (124b)
kṣaṇāttu kiṃcidadhikamabhyasettu dinedine
valī ca palitaṃ caiva ṣaṇmāsārdhānna dṛśyate (125)
yāmamātraṃ tu yo nityamabhyasetsa tu kālajit (126a)

Anvay
prathame dine: on the first day; *śiraḥ*: head; *syāt*: should be; *adhaḥ*: on the ground; *ca*: and; *pādaḥ*: his legs; *ūrdhva*: raised up; *kṣanam*: for a moment; *dine dine*: every day; *abhyaset*: he should practise; *kiṃcit-adhikam kṣaṇāt*: a little longer; *valī*: wrinkles; *ca eva*: and even; *palitam*: grey hair; *na dṛśyate*: will not be seen; *saṇmā sa ardhāt*: after six and a half [months]; *tu*: indeed; *yaḥ*: whoever; *abhyaset*: practises; *nityam*: continuously; *mātram*: for a period; *yāma*: of three hours; *jit*: conquers; *kāla*: time.

Translation
On the first day [his] head should be on the ground and [his] legs raised up for a moment. Every day he should practise a little longer. Wrinkles and even grey hair will not be seen after six and a half months. Indeed, whoever practises continuously for a period of three hours conquers time.

Commentary
Viparīta karaṇī mudrā is a powerful practice due to the inverted position of the body. All the energy which would normally flow downward towards the feet due to the upright posture and the pull of gravity, is induced to flow in the opposite direction, into the head. Therefore, in this verse, it is recommended that one should develop the practice slowly.

On the first day the legs should be raised over the head and held in this position for a moment. Every day the duration of the practice can be increased a little longer. Viparīta karaṇī mudrā is described in the classical yogic texts as a rejuvenating practice. Due to the pressure placed on the base of the neck, while the legs are raised, this practice activates viśuddhi cakra, which is also known as the center of rejuvenation, the internal fountain of youth.

Bindu and viśuddhi cakras are linked due to the nectar connection. The *amṛta*, or nectar of life, is said to drip down slowly from bindu cakra throughout the duration of one's life. The nectar passes down through the region of the head without being absorbed, and collects at viśuddhi chakra. The nectar of life also contains *viś*, or 'poison', which is responsible for the processes of aging, disease and death. Hence the nectar of life also holds the cycle of disease and death within it.

The word viśuddhi has two roots, viś plus *śuddhi*, which means 'purification'. Hence, viśuddhi cakra is the purification center for the viś, or poison, contained within the nectar.

However, this process may only be carried out, if viśuddhi has been activated. In most people, viśuddhi remains relatively dormant, and so the nectar passes through it without being purified of the vish, or poison. This becomes the on-going cause of aging, disease and death in the body. In order to reverse this cycle of degeneration, viśuddhi cakra must be activated for extended periods on a regular basis. This is the main reason why the yogis of old performed viparīta karaṇī mudrā is a powerful practice due to the inverted position of the body. All the energy which would normally flow downward towards the feet due to the upright posture and the pull of gravity, is induced to flow in the opposite direction, into the head. Therefore, in this verse, it is recommended that one should develop the practice slowly. They found that by slowly increasing the duration of the practice, after six months, wrinkles and grey hair would disappear. The yogi would be endowed with youth and vitality. Furthermore, by extending the practice for a period of three hours on a regular basis they were able to transcend time and space, and experience the universal state of consciousness.

Verses 126b and 127: Benefits of vajrolī

वज्रोलीमभ्यसेद्यस्तु स योगी सिद्धिभाजनम् ।।१२६।।
लभ्यते यदि तस्यैव योगसिद्धिः करे स्थिता ।
अतीतानागतं वेत्ति खेचरी च भवेद्ध्रुवम् ।।१२७।।
vajrolīmabhyasedyastu sa yogī siddhibhājanam (126b)
labhyate yadi tasyaiva yogasiddhiḥ karesthitā
atītānāgataṃ vetti khecarī ca bhaveddhruvam (127)

Anvay
tu: indeed; *yaḥ*: whoever; *abhyaset*: practises; *vajrolīm*: contraction and release of the urinary passage; *yogī*: yogin; *bhājanam*: recipient; *siddhi*: of psychic powers; *yadi*: if; *yoga-siddhiḥ*: accomplishment in *yoga*; *eva*: ever; *labhyate*: is attained; *tasya*: by him; *kare sthitā*: it is lasting; *vetti*: he knows; *āgatam*: events; *atītān*: of the past; *ca*: and; *dhruvam*: certainly; *bhavet*: has; *khecarī*: power of flight.

Translation
Indeed whoever practises vajrolī is a yogin [and] the recipient of siddhis. If accomplishment in yoga is ever attained by him, it is lasting. He knows the events of the past and certainly has the power of flight.

Commentary
Vajrolī is an important mudrā, which involves direct contraction of the urethra. When practised regularly, it redirects the energy in the swādhiṣṭhāna cakra region upward to the brain. Swādhiṣṭhāna is the center for sexual pleasure and procreation. If the energy remains in this region, it will cause attraction towards these pursuits and will ultimately be lost in emission. By redirecting this energy upward, the higher centers of viśuddhi, ajña and bindu are suffused with prāṇa and become activated.

The definition of a yogi is 'one who is accomplished in yoga'. In order to be accomplished in yoga, the higher centers must be activated, which allows one to live in the subtle states of consciousness.

The verse further states that should a practitioner of vajrolī ever attain accomplishment in yoga, that mastery will be permanent. There will be no fall from or loss of this level of realization. Such a yogi will have the power to see the events of the past. He will also be able to leave the physical body at will and move about freely in the astral form.

Verses 128 and 129a: Amarolī and vajrolī

अमरीं यः पिबेन्नित्यं नस्यं कुर्वन्दिने ।
वज्रोलीमभ्यसेन्नित्यममरोलीति कथ्यते ।।१२८।।
ततो भवेद्राजयोगो नान्तरा भवति ध्रुवम् ।१२९।
amarīṃ yaḥ pibennityaṃ nasyaṃ kurvandine
vajrolīmabhyasennityamamarolīti kathyate (128)
tato bhavedrājayogo nāntarā bhavati dhruvam (129a)

Anvay
yaḥ: whoever; *nityam*: always; *pibet*: drinks; *amarīm*: amarolī, midstream of urine; *dine*: daily; *kurvan*: taking; *nasyam*: through the nose; *nityam*: always; *abhyaset*: practises; *vajrolīm*: contraction and release of urinary passage; *kathyate*: he is said; *amarolī*: drinking of one's own urine for detoxification, stamina, vitality and immunity; *tataḥ*: then; *bhavet*: he attains; *rājayogaḥ*: royal path of yoga, leading to enlightenment through meditation; *bhavati*: there is; *dhruvam*: certainly; *na*: no; *antarā*: distance.

Translation
Whoever always drinks the mid-stream of urine daily, taking [it] through the nose, [and] always practises vajrolī, is said [to be a practitioner of] amarolī. Then he attains rāja yoga, [and] there is certainly no distance [between him and enlightenment].

Commentary
Amarolī is the yogic practice of drinking the mid-stream of one's first urination in the early morning, upon awakening. The word *amara* means 'free from death' or 'undying'. One's own urine contains many minerals and enzymes, which are particularly suitable to one's body. Normally, these valuable nutrients would be lost during urination, but in this practice they are re-consumed. Only the mid-stream of the first urination should be collected in a glass.

This urine may then be drunk through the mouth, or sniffed through the nose and swallowed. Taking it through the nose has many benefits, as it clears the muscus membranes and sinuses of accumulated mucus and bacteria.

When amarolī is performed along with vajrolī mudrā every day regularly over a long duration of time, the body is revitalised and the prāṇas are redirected upward. This shift in the energy influences the mind and consciousness, and is conducive for meditation. Rāja yoga is the yoga of meditation. Hence, the verse says that this practitioner attains rāja yoga, and there is no distance; the practitioner arrives at the goal, and becomes an enlightened yogi.

Verses 129b, 130 and 131a: Kriyās of rāja yoga

यदा तु राजयोगेन निष्पन्ना योगिभिः क्रिया ।।१२९।।
तदा विवेकवैराग्यं जायते योगिनो ध्रुवम् ।
विष्णुर्नाम महायोगी महाभूतो महातपाः ।।१३०।।
तत्त्वमार्गे तथा दीपो दृश्यते पुरुषोत्तमः ।१३१।
yadā tu rājayogena niṣpannā yogibhiḥ kriyā (129b)
tadā vivekavairāgyaṃ jāyate yogino dhruvam
viṣṇurnāma mahāyogī mahābhūto mahātapāḥ (130)
tattvamārge tathā dīpo dṛśyate puruṣottamaḥ (131a)

Anvay

yadā: when; *kriyā*: spiritual activity due to yogic practices; *niṣpannā*: is brought about; *yogibhiḥ*: by yogins; *rājayogena*: through rāja yoga; *tadā*: then; *yoginaḥ*: yogins; *dhruvam*: certainly; *jāyate*: are victorious in; *viveka*: *viveka*, discrimination between the permanent and impermanent; *vairagya*: non-attachment to the material world; *puruṣottamaḥ*: Supreme Spirit; *viṣṇuḥ*: preserver of the universe; *mahāyogī*: great yogin; *mahābhūtaḥ*: lord of the elements; *mahātapāḥ*: master of austerities; *tathā*: then; *dṛśyate*: is seen; *dīpaḥ*: as a light; *mārge*: on the path; *tattva*: of the true reality.

Translation

When kriyā is brought about by yogins through rāja yoga, then the yogins are certainly victorious in *viveka* and *vairagya.* The supreme spirit, Viṣṇu, who is the great yogin, lord of the elements and master of austerities, is then seen as a light on the path of the true reality.

Commentary

The kriyās, spiritual actions, of haṭha yoga, kriyā yoga and rāja yoga, are different. The kriyās of haṭha yoga and kriyā yoga involve different combinations of āsana, prāṇāyāma, mudrā and bandha, for the awakening of the cakras and the kuṇḍalinī energies. However, the kriyās of rāja yoga, as described in the 'Yoga Sutras of Patañjali', are spiritual disciplines, such as: *tapas* (austeritiy), *swadhyaya* (self-study) and *īśwara praṇidhāna* (faith in or dedication to the highest reality).

Tapas, austerity, is an important spiritual discipline and practice, because it purifies and strengthens the body and mind, making one capable of sustaining higher levels of energy and consciousness. Swadhyaya, self-study, is necessary for all yogic practitioners, as it redirects the attention from the outer phenomenal world to inner world of the body, mind and consciousness. It is self-awareness that leads to self-realization. Īśwara praṇidhāna, faith in a higher reality beyond oneself, is a requisite of yoga. Without faith in and dedication to a higher reality, there can be no ultimate aim or purpose in yoga, or even in life itself.

When these three kriyās of rāja yoga become an integral part of one's spiritual practice, the yogi develops *viveka* and *vairagya*, the spiritual attributes of yoga. Viveka means 'discrimination', the ability to know truth from untruth, permanent from impermanent, reality from illusion. This kind of discrimination is not only intellectual, but experiential. One knows the truth, because one has experienced it within one's own self. Vairagya, non-attachment, is a natural outcome of viveka. One who knows the reality, will no longer be attracted or attached to the ephemeral objects and relationships of the world.

Viṣṇu is a name or symbol that is used by yogis to represent the supreme, universal consciousness. Viṣṇu, the supreme consciousness, is the goal of yogis, and so is considered here to be the great yogin, himself. Viṣṇu is the lord of all the elements, because consciousness is the source of all material existence, and all material existence is comprised of elements. Viṣṇu is also considered to be the master of all austerities, because intentional hardship is an act of imposing the conscious will over the body and mind. Normally, in worldly life, the body and mind exert their influence over the consciousness. In this way, the yogi perceives Viṣṇu, the supreme consciousness, as light, illumining the pathway of the ultimate reality.

Verses 131b, 132, 133 and 134a: Wheel of saṃsāra

यः स्तनः पूर्वपीतस्तं निष्पीड्य मुदमश्नुते ।।१३१।।
यस्माज्जातो भगात्पूर्वं तस्मिन्नेव भगे रमन् ।
या माता सा पुनर्भार्या या भार्या मातरेव हि ।।१३२।।
यः पिता स पुनः पुत्रो यः पुत्रः स पुनः पिता ।
एवं संसारचक्रेण कूपचक्रे घटा इव ।।१३३।।
भ्रमन्तो योनिजन्मानि श्रुत्वा लोकान्समश्नुते ।१३४।

yaḥ stanaḥ pūrvapītastaṃ niṣpīḍya mudamaśnute (131b)
yasmājjāto bhagātpūrvaṃ tasminneva bhage raman
yā mātā sā punarbhāryā yā bhāryā mātareva hi (132)
yaḥ pitā sa punaḥ putro yaḥ putraḥ sa punaḥ pitā
evaṃ saṃsāracakreṇa kūpacakre ghaṭā iva (133)
bhramanto yonijanmāni śrutvā lokānsamaśnute (134a)

Anvay

yaḥ: that; *stanaḥ*: breast; *pītaḥ*: [from which] he drank; *pūrva*: before; *aśnute*: he obtains; *mudam*: joy; *niṣpīḍya*: by fondling; *raman*: he delights; *tasmin eva bhage*: in that very organ; *yasmāt*: from which; *jātaḥ*: he was born; *pūrvam*: previously; *yā*: she who; *bhāryā*: wife; *eva*: now; *mātā*: mother; *sā*: she; *punaḥ*: again; *sa yaḥ*: he who; *pitā*: father; *punaḥ*: again; *putraḥ*: son; *śrutvā*: hearing; *samaśnute*: he abides in; *lokān*: worlds; *evam*: in the same way as; *yonijanmāni*: beings; *bhramantaḥ*: wandering; *saṃsāra-cakreṇa*: through the wheel of birth, death and rebirth; *iva*: like; *ghaṭā*: jar; *kūpacakre*: in a water-wheel.

Translation

That breast from which he drank before, he obtains joy by fondling, [and] he delights in that very organ from which he was previously born. She who was his wife is now his mother, and she who is now his mother will again be his wife. He who is the father will again be the son, and he who is the son will again be the father. Hearing [this], he abides in the worlds, in the same way as the beings wandering through the wheel of *saṃsāra*, like a jar in a water-wheel.

Commentary

These verses allude to the purpose of yoga, which is ultimately to be liberated from the wheel of saṃsāra. Worldly life, or saṃsāra, is symbolized by a wheel, which turns around and around continuously, always coming back to the same point and then going around again. The wheel of saṃsāra is based upon the law of karma. Every action has an effect, which becomes the cause of another action. Every rotation of the wheel is followed by another, due to the relentless momentum of karma. As long as there is karma within the mind of an individual, the wheel of saṃsāra continues to turn, and one is hopelessly bound to it.

The wheel of saṃsāra is very aptly described here. The breast from which the infant son greedily drinks, later becomes an object of allurement, which the youth fondles with great joy. The birth canal, from which he was previously born, later becomes a source of pure delight, which he seeks again and again to penetrate. In his last birth, the woman who was his wife, now becomes his mother. In his next birth, she who is now his mother, will again become his wife. Similarly, he who is now the father, will next become the son, and he who is the son, will again become the father.

Understanding this, the yogi abides in the material world, like other beings, wandering around the wheel of saṃsāra, like a clay pot attached to a water wheel. The yogi also lives in the physical body, like other people, and is susceptible to the karmas and influences of the world. But the difference is that he realizes this, and takes great care to revolve around the wheel, without creating further karmas and attachments. He understands the fragility of life, which is easily and quickly broken, like a clay pot, and utilitizes it to obtain emancipation, rather than future births in saṃsāra.

Verses 134b, 135 and 136a: Power of Aum

त्रयो लोकास्त्रयो वेदास्तिस्रः संध्यास्त्रय: स्वराः ।।१३४।।
त्रयो ऽग्नयश्च त्रिगुणा: स्थिताः सर्वे त्रयाक्षरे ।
त्रयाणामक्षराणां च यो ऽधीते ऽप्यर्धमक्षरम् ।।१३५।।
तेन सर्वमिदं प्रोतं तत्सत्यं तत्परं पदम् ।१३६।
trayo lokāstrayo vedāstisraḥ saṃdhyāstrayaḥ svarāḥ (134b)
trayo 'gnayaśca triguṇāḥ sthitāḥ sarve trayākṣare
trayāṇāmakṣarāṇāṃ ca yo 'dhīte 'pyardhamakṣaram (135)
tena sarvamidaṃ protaṃ tatsatyaṃ tatparaṃ padam (136a)

Anvay
trayaḥ lokāḥ: three worlds; *trayaḥ vedāḥ*: three *Vedas*, sacred knowledge of the *Rig Veda, Sāma Veda* and *Yajur Veda*; *tisraḥ saṃdhyāḥ*: three time junctures of the day when spiritual practices were performed at dawn, noon and dusk; *trayaḥ svarāḥ*: three swara; *trayaḥ agnayaḥ*: three fires; *ca*: and; *triguṇāḥ*: three qualities of nature; *sarve*: all; *sthitāḥ*: are placed; *traya-akṣare*: in the three imperishable sounds; *ca*: and; *yaḥ*: whoever; *adhīte*: has delved into; *api*: even; *ardham-akṣaram*: half a sound; *protam*: is pervaded by; *sarvam-idam*: all this; *tat*: this; *satyam*: Truth; *tat*: this; *param*: Supreme; *padam*: Seat.

Translation
The three worlds, three Vedas, three *sandhyās*, three *swaras*, three fires and the three *guṇas* are all placed in the three imperishable sounds [of *Aum*], and whoever has delved into even half a sound is pervaded by all this. This [is] the Truth; this [is] the Supreme Seat.

Commentary
The mantra *Aum* is the primal sound, the first vibration of creation. The Upaniṣads extoll this mantra and prescribe meditation upon it to attain the highest states of

consciousness and self-realization. Being the first vibration, meditation on this pure sound brings the mind back to the source of being. Any other method or object of meditation falls short of this premise, because Aum is the first, and all other sounds and forms come after it. Even in the Bible it is said that 'in the beginning was the word, and the word was with God, and the word was God'. Aum is that first word, first sound, that issued directly from the cosmic consciousness. From Aum all other sound vibrations emanated, and from sound vibrations came all forms, all the entities and beings in the manifest universe.

The sound of *Aum* represents the unity of all existence. However, it is comprised of three *mātrās*, or letters: A, U and M, which symbolize the trinity and hence the multiplicity of all created existence. Creation comes into existence due to the different trinities: (i) the three worlds, (ii) the three Vedas, (iii) the three *sandhyās*, (iv) the three *swaras*, (v) the three *agnis* and (vi) the three *guṇas*. The three worlds are the planes of: earth, purgatory and heaven. The three Vedas, which represent all knowledge, are the: Rig Veda, Sāma Veda and Yajur Veda. The three sandhyās, are the important periods of changeover during the day, which are often used for spiritual practice: ten minutes before and after dawn, ten minutes before and after midday, and ten minutes before and after dusk. The three swaras are the major energy channels in the body: *iḍā* (mental energy), *piṅgalā* (vital energy) and *suṣumnā* (spiritual energy). The three fires are the sources of light: fire, which burns on earth, lightening, which illumines the sky, and the sun, which shines down from the heavens. The three guṇas are the qualities inherent in all nature: *tamas*, stability, *rajas*, movement, and *sattwa*, balance.

The verse states that all of the six trinities have their source in the three imperishable sounds A, U and M, which comprise the mantra *Aum*. And furthermore, any aspirant who contemplates these sounds, and experiences even half of one sound, is filled with the knowledge of all these trinities. This is the truth, because Aum is the supreme seat. All the trinities of creation issue from this one primal sound, and ultimately all return to this one source.

Verses 136b, 137, 138 and 139a: Meditation on Aum in the heart lotus

पुष्पमध्ये यथा गन्धः पयोमध्ये यथा घृतम् ।।१३६।।
तिलमध्ये यथा तैलं पाषाणेष्विव काञ्चनम् ।
हृदि स्थाने स्थितं पद्मं तस्य वक्रमधोमुखम् ।।१३७।।
ऊर्ध्वनालमधोबिन्दुस्तस्य मध्ये स्थितं मनः ।
अकारे रेचितं पद्ममुकारेणैव भिद्यते ।।१३८।।
मकारे लभते नादमर्धमात्रा तु निश्चला ।१३९।
puṣpamadhye yathā gandhaḥ payomadhye yathā ghṛtam 136b
tilamadhye yathā tailam pāṣāṇeṣviva kāñcanam
hṛdi sthāne sthitaṃ padmaṃ tasya vakramadhomukham (137)
ūrdhvanālamadhobindustasya madhye sthitaṃ manaḥ
akāre recitaṃ padmamukāreṇaiva bhidyate (138)
makāre labhate nādamardhamātrā tu niścalā (139a)

Anvay
yathā: as; *gandhaḥ*: fragrance; *madhye*: within; *puṣpa*: flower; *yathā*: as; *ghṛtam*: ghee; *madhye*: within; *payaḥ*: milk; *yathā*: as; *tailam*: oil; *madhye*: within; *tilam*: sesame; *iva*: like; *kāñcanam*: gold; *pāṣāṇeṣu*: in rocks; *padmam*: lotus; *sthitam*: is placed; *sthāne*: in the area; *hṛdi*: of the heart; *tasya*: its; *mukham*: face; *vakram*: bent; *adhaḥ*: down; *nālam*: stalk; *ūrdhva*: upright; *tasya*: its; *binduḥ*: seed, source; *adhaḥ*: below; *madhye*: within; *sthitam*: abides; *manaḥ*: mind, intelligent principle; *padmam*: lotus; *recitam*: is expanded; *akāre*: with the sound A; *ukāreṇa*: with the sound U; *bhidyate*: is opened up; *makāre*: by the sound M; *labhate*: it obtains; *nādam*: inner sound of *Aum*; *ardhamātrā*: half syllable; *niścalā*: still.

Translation
As the fragrance within the flower, as the ghee within the milk, as the oil within the sesame, as the gold within the

rock, [so] is the lotus placed in the area of the heart. Its face is bent down; its stalk is upright. Its *bindu* is below; within it abides *manas*. The lotus is expanded with the sound A; with the sound U, it is opened up; by the sound M, it obtains sound, and the half syllable is still.

Commentary

The power of *Aum* can only be realised by the aspirant through diligent practice of meditation. The sound of *Aum* is heard within the inner recesses of the heart. The heart is the abode of the *jīvātma*, the living soul. This is why the *Aum* sound can be heard in the lotus of the heart. Just as fragrance is the subtle essence of the flower, ghee the inherent richness within milk, oil the extract of sesame, and gold the quintessence of rock; similarly, the lotus is the subtle essence of the heart. Here the lotus represents *anāhata cakra*, the psychic energy center, located in heart region. Anāhata comes from the root *anāhad,* which means 'unstruck'. Unstruck refers to that *nāda*, or inner sound, which is not produced by the friction of two or more objects, as occurs with external sound.

When the anāhata lotus is dormant, it remains closed and faces downward. The closed lotus is fixed on the upright stalk of suṣumnā, the spiritual energy channel. Because the lotus faces downwards, its bindu, or central point, is below. Anāhata cakra is associated with the principle of *manas*, or mind, and is connected with the intelligence of the heart. When the aspirant meditates on the three syllables of *Aum* in the heart, the lotus expands with the sound 'A'. With the sound 'U' the lotus turns upward and opens. With the vibration 'M' the inner sound of Aum is complete, and resonates as nāda, the subtle, inner sound. The sound 'M' is actually a half letter, *ardhamātrā*, and so it is represented by a bindu or point. By following this point, the aspirant is lead deep within the inner consciousness to the state of absolute stillness, from which the *Aum* sound issues.

Verses 139b, 140a: Final realization of yoga

शुद्धस्फटिकसंकाशं निष्कलं पापनाशनम् ।।१३९।।
लभते योगयुक्तात्मा पुरुषसस्तत्परं पदम् ।१४०।
śuddhasphaṭikasaṃkāśaṃ niṣkalaṃ pāpanāśanam (139b)
labhate yogayuktātmā puruṣastatparaṃ padam (140a)

Anvay
puruṣaḥ: person; *ātmā*: self; *yoga-yukta*: is united with yoga; *labhate*: obtains; *tat-param padam*: that supreme seat; *saṃkāśam*: has the appearance of; *śuddha-sphaṭika*: pure crystal; *niṣkalaam*: undivided; *nāśanam*: destroys; *pāpa*: sins.

Translation
The person whose self is united with yoga obtains that supreme seat, [which] has the appearance of pure crystal, [is] undivided [and] destroys sins.

Commentary
Anāhata lotus, the heart center, is where meditation is practised. However, *sahasrāra*, the crown center, is where the highest meditation is ultimately realized. The person who has merged with his own ātmā, or pure consciousness, is united in yoga and has reached that supreme seat. Sahasrāra is the thousand petalled lotus, which extends like a thousand rays of light into the cosmic consciousness. At the center of this lotus is the crystal liṅgam, or symbol of pure transcendence. Sahasrāra is the center of the unmanifest, unborn consciousness, and so it is not influenced by or associated with any diversity, relating with name or form, in the dimension of time and space. Hence it is the One, undivided, essence of consciousness and existence. Being beyond all evolutes and phenomenon, sahasrara is beyond all duality, and thus beyond all sin. Being beyond sin, there is no sin that can exist within it. Therefore, its proximity is said to destroy all sin.

Verses 140b, 141 and 142: The stillness of kumbhaka

कूर्मः स्वपाणिपादादिशिरश्चात्मनि धारयेत् ।।१४०।।
एवं द्वारेषु सर्वेषु वायुपूरितरेचितः ।
निषिद्धे तु नवद्वारे ऊर्ध्वं प्राङ्निश्वसंस्तथा ।।१४१।।
घटमध्ये यथा दीपो निवातं कुम्भकं विदुः ।
निषिद्धैर्नवभिर्वीरैर्निर्जने निरुपद्रवे ।।१४२।।
kūrmaḥ svapāṇipādādiśiraścātmani dhārayet (140b)
evaṃ dvāreṣu sarveṣu vāyupūritarecitaḥ
niṣiddhe tu navadvāre ūrdhvaṃ prāṅniśvasaṃstathā (141)
ghaṭamadhye yathā dīpo nivātaṃ kumbhakaṃ viduḥ
niṣiddhairnavabhirvīrairnirjane nirupadrave (142)

Anvay
kūrmaḥ: tortoise; *dhārayet*: holds; *ātmani*: within itself; *sva-pāṇi*: its own hands; *pāda*: feet; *ca . . ādi*: and . . also; *śiraḥ*: head; *evam*: so; *vāyu*: air; *pūrita*: is inhaled; *recitaḥ*: exhaled; *sarveṣu dvāreṣu*: in all the orifices [of the body]; *tathā*: then; *niśvasam*: drawing in the breath; *prāṅ*: forwards; *ūrdhvam*: upwards; *nava-dvāre*: nine orifices; *niṣiddhe*: are restrained; *yathā*: like; *dīpaḥ*: lamp; *madhye*: inside; *ghaṭa*: jar; *nivātam*: stillness; *kumbhakam*: breath retention; *viduḥ*: is known; *vīraiḥ*: by adepts; *niṣiddhaiḥ*: who have restrained; *navabhiḥ*: nine orifices; *nirjane*: in a deserted place; *nirupadrave*: free from disturbances.

Translation
The tortoise holds within itself its own hands, feet and also head, so is the air inhaled and exhaled in all the orifices [of the body]. Then, drawing in the breath forwards and upwards, when the nine orifices are restrained, like a lamp inside a jar, the stillness of kumbhaka is known by adepts, who have restrained the nine orifices in a deserted place, free from disturbances.

Commentary
Just as the tortoise withdraws its head and four limbs within itself, similarly the yogi withdraws the five senses back into the mind. When the five senses are allowed to roam freely in the external world, that is sensory awareness. When the five senses are withdrawn back into the mind and restrained for a period of time, that is the state of *pratyāhāra*, the first level of meditation. In pratyāhāra, the mind is nourished by the subtle sensory impressions, which are accumulated in the mind. At this time the body continues to breathe in and out, and the nine orifices remain open. The nine orifices are the points where the body is open to the external world: the two eyes, the two ears, the two nostrils, the mouth, the anal sphincter and the urinary opening.

In order to enter the higher states of meditation, yogis took recourse to the practice of kumbhaka, breath retention. In the *Yoga Sūtras of Patañjali*, it says that kumbhaka leads to dhārana, the state of concentration. Dhāraṇā is the second level of meditation, where the impressions of the mind begin to thin, and it is possible to focus on one object alone. In the above verse, internal kumbhaka is described for this purpose. Drawing the breath forward and upward refers to the inhalation. After inhalation, the breath is retained, and the nine orifices are restrained. In this way, the mind remains absolutely still, just like a lamp inside a jar.

When a flame is lit outside in the open air, it will flicker and waver continuously. Similarly, when the senses are exposed to the outside world, they will pull the mind hither and thither, from one object to another, ceaselessly. However, when the senses are withdrawn into the mind, and then restrained by the practice of kumbhaka, breath retention, the mind becomes absolutely still. This is not an imaginary experience or a hallucination. It is based on a scientific fact, that when the breath stops, the mind also stops. As long as the breath continues to flow, the mind remains active. This was well known to the adepts of yoga, who perfected mind control through the practice of kumbhaka in deserted places, free from disturbances.

Conclusion

निश्चितं त्वात्ममात्रेणावशिष्टं योगसेवया ।।
इत्युपनिषत् ।।
niścitaṃ tvātmamātreṇāvaśiṣṭaṃ yogasevayā
ityupaniṣat

Anvay
yoga-sevayā: through dedication to *yoga*; *tva*: you; *niścitam*: surely; *ātma*:, supreme consciousness; *mātreṇa*: alone; *avaśiṣṭam*: remains; *iti*: thus; *upaniṣat*: ancient sacred text.

Translation
Through dedication to yoga, you surely [will realise] that the atma, the highest consciousness, alone remains. Thus ends the Upaniṣad.

Commentary
Yoga may be written about and discoursed in the upaniṣads and in other philosophical texts. However, the essence of yoga is not to be understood verbally or intellectually. Yoga is an experiential science; it is the science of the *ātmā*, the self. The self of every person is not the ego, the psyche or the mind; these are merely its evolutes. The self is the pure field of consciousness, which transcends the mind and its individual world of comings and goings. Through dedication to the practice of yoga, you will surely realize in the stillness of your being that only your pure consciousness remains, and you are That.

Thus [ends] the Upaniṣad.

APPENDICES

1. Sanskrit text

योगतत्त्वं प्रवक्ष्यामि योगिनां हितकाम्यया ।
यच्छुत्वा च पठितवा च सर्वपापैः प्रमुच्यते ।।१।।

विष्णुर्नाम महायोगो महाभूतो महातपाः ।
तत्त्वमार्गे यथा दोपो दृश्यते पुरुषोत्तमः ।।२।।

तमाराध्य जगन्नाथं प्रणिपत्य पितामः ।
पप्रच्छ योगतत्त्वं मे ब्रूहि चाष्टाङ्गसंयुतम् ।।३।।

तमुवाच हृषोकेशो वक्ष्यामि शृणु तत्त्वतः ।
सर्वे जोवाः सुखैर्दुःखैर्मायाजालेन वेष्टिताः ।।४।।

तेषां मुकतिकरं मार्गं मायाजालनिकृन्तनम् ।
जन्ममृत्युजराव्याधिनाशनं मृत्युतारकम् ।।५।।

नानामार्गैस्तु दुष्प्रापं कैवल्यं परमं पदम् ।
पतिताः शास्त्रजालेषु प्रज्ञया तेन मोहिताः ।।६।।

अनिर्वाच्यं पदं वक्तुं न शक्यं तैः सुरैरपि ।
स्वात्मप्रकाशरूपं तत्किं शास्त्रेण प्रकाश्यते ।।७।।

निष्कलं निर्मलं शान्तं सार्वातोतं निरामयं ।
तदेव जोवरूपेण पुण्यपापफलैर्वृतम् ।।८।।

परमात्मपदं नित्यं तात्कथं जोवतां गतम् ।
सर्वभावपदातोतं ज्ञानरूपं निरञ्जनम् ।।९।।

वारिवात्स्फुरितं तासमिस्तात्राहंकृतिरुत्थिता ।
पञ्चात्मकमभूत्पिण्डं धातुबद्धं गुणात्मकम् ।।१०।।

सुखदु:खै: समायुक्तं जोवभावनया कुरु ।
तेन जोवाभिधा प्रोक्ता विशुद्धै: परमात्मनि ।।११।।

कामक्रोधभयं चापि मोहलोभमदो रज: ।
जन्म मृत्युश्च कर्पन्यं शोकस्तन्द्रा क्षुधातृषा ।।१२।।

तृष्णा लज्जा भयं दु:ख: विषादो हर्ष एव च ।
एभिर्दोषैर्विनिर्मुक्त: स जोव: केवलो मत: ।।१३।।

तस्माद्दोषविनाशार्थमुपाय: कथयामि ते ।
योगहीनं कथं ज्ञानं मोक्षदं भवति ध्रुवम् ।।१४।।

योगो हि ज्ञानहीनस्तु न क्षमो मोक्षकर्मणि ।
तस्माज्ज्ञानं च योगं च मुमुक्षुर्द्दढम्यसेत् ।।१५।।

अज्ञानादेव संसारो ज्ञानादेव विमुच्यते ।
ज्ञानस्वरूपमेवादौ ज्ञानं ज्ञेयैकसाधनम् ।।१६।।

ज्ञातं येन निजं रूपं कैवल्यं परमं पदम् ।
निष्कलं निर्मलं साक्षात्सच्चिदानन्दरूपकम् ।।१७।।

उत्पत्तिस्थितिसंहारस्फूर्तिज्ञानविवीर्जतम् ।
एतज्ज्ञानमिति परोक्तमथ योगं ब्रवीमि ते ।।१८।।

योगो हि बहुधा ब्रह्मन्भिद्यते व्यवहारत: ।
मन्त्रयोगो लयश्चैव हठो ऽसौ राजयोगत: ।।१९।।

आरम्भश्च घटश्चैव तथा परिचय: स्मृत: ।
निष्पत्तिश्चेत्यवस्था च सर्वत्र परिकीर्तिता ।।२०।।

एतेषा: लक्षणं ब्रह्मन्वक्ष्ये शृणु समासत: ।
मातृकादियुतं मन्त्रं द्वादशाब्दं तु यो जपेत् ।।२१।।

क्रमेण लभते ज्ञानमणिमादिगुणान्वितम् ।

अल्पबुद्धिरिमं योगं सेवते साधकाधमः ।।२२।।

लययोगश्चित्तलयः कोटिशः परिकीर्तितः ।
गच्छन्तिष्ठन्स्वपन्भुञ्जन्ध्यायेन्निष्कलमीश्वरम् ।।२३।।

स एव लययोगः स्याद्धहठयोगमतः शृणु ।
यमश्च नियमशचैव आसनं प्राणसंयमः ।।२४।।

प्रत्याहारो धारणा च ध्यानं भ्रूमध्यं हरिम् ।
समाधिः समतावस्था साष्टाङ्गो योग उच्यते ।।२५।।

महामुद्रा महाबन्धः महावेधश्च खेचरी ।
जालंधरोड्डियाणश्च मूलबन्धस्तथैव च ।।२६।।

दीर्घप्रणवसंधानं सिद्धान्तश्रवणं परम् ।
वज्रोली चामरोली च सहजोली त्रिधामता ।।२७।।

एतेषां लक्षणं ब्रह्मन्प्रत्येकं शृणु तत्त्वतः ।
लघ्वाहारो यमेष्वेको मुख्यो भवति नेतरः ।।२८।।

अहिंसा नियमेष्वेका मुख्या वै चतुरानन ।
सिद्धं पद्मं तथा सिंहं भद्रं चेति चतुष्टयम् ।।२९।।

प्रथमाभ्यासकाले तु विघ्नः स्युश्चतुरानन् ।
आलस्य कत्थनं धूर्तगोष्टी मन्त्रादिसाधनम् ।।३०।।

धातुस्त्रीलौल्यकादीनि मृगतृष्णामायानि वै ।
ज्ञात्वा सुधीस्त्यजेत्सर्वान्विघ्नान्पुण्यप्रभावतः ।।३१।।

प्राणायामं ततः कुर्यात्पद्मासनगतः स्वयम् ।
सुशोभनं मठं कुर्यात्सूक्ष्मद्वारं तु निर्व्रणम् ।।३२।।

सुस्थुं लिप्तं गोमयेन सुधया वा प्रयत्नतः ।
मत्कुनैर्मशकैर्लूतैर्वर्जितं च प्रयत्नतः ।।३३।।

दिने दिने च संमृष्टं समार्जन्या विशेसत: ।
वासितं च सुगन्धेन धूपितं गुग्गुलादिभि: ।।३४।।

नात्युच्छ्रितं नातिनीचं चैलाजिनकुशोत्तरम् ।
तत्रोपविश्य मेधावी पद्मासनसमन्वित: ।।३५।।

ऋजुकाय: प्राञ्जलिश्च प्रणमेदिष्टदेवताम ।
ततो दक्षिणहस्तस्य अङ्गष्ठेनैव पिङ्गलाम् ।।३६।।

निरुध्य पूरयेद्वायुमिडया तु शनै: शनै: ।
यथाशक्त्यविरोधेन तत: कुर्याच्च कुम्भकम ।।३७।।

पुनस्त्यजेत्पिङ्गलया शनैरेव न वेगत: ।
पुन: पिङ्गलयापूर्य पूरयेदुदरं शनै: ।।३८।।

धारयित्वा यथाशक्ति रेचयेदिदया शनै: ।
यया त्यजेत्तयापूर्य धारयेदविरोधत: ।।३९।।

जानु प्रदक्षिणीकृत्य न द्रुतं न विलम्बितम् ।
अङ्गुलिस्फोटनं कुर्यात्सा मात्रा परिगीयते ।।४०।।

इडया वायुमारोप्य शनै: षोडशमात्रया ।
कुम्भयेत्पूरितं पश्चाच्चतु: षष्ट्या तु मात्रया ।।४१।।

रेचयेत्पिङ्गलानाड्या द्वात्रिंशन्मात्रया पुन: ।
पुन: पिङ्गलयापूर्य पूर्ववत्सुसमाहित: ।।४२।।

प्रातर्मध्याम्दिने सायमर्धरात्रे च कुम्भकान् ।
शनैरशीतिपर्यन्तं चतुर्वारं समभ्यसेत् ।।४३।।

एवं मासत्रयाभ्यासान्नाडीशुद्धिस्ततो भवेत् ।
यदा तु नाडीशुद्धि: स्यात्तदा चिह्नानि बाह्यत: ।।४४।।

जायन्ते योगिनो देहे तानि वक्ष्याम्यशेसतः ।
शरीरलघुता दीप्तिर्जाठराग्निविवर्धनम् ।।४५।।

कृशत्वं च शरीरस्य तदा जायेत निश्चितम् ।
योगविघ्नकराहारं वर्जयेद्योगवित्तमः ।।४६।।

लवणं सर्षपं चाम्लमुष्णं रूक्षं च तीक्ष्णकम् ।
शाकजातं रामठादि वह्निस्त्रीपथसेवनम् ।।४७।।

प्रातः स्नानोपवासादिकायक्लेशाम्श्च वर्जयेत् ।
अभ्यासकाले प्रथमं शस्तं क्षीराज्यभोजनम् ।।४८।।

गोधूममुद्गशाल्यन्नं योगवृद्धिकरं विदुः ।
ततः परं यथेष्टं तु शक्तः स्याद्वायुधारणे ।।४९।।

यथेष्टधारणाद्वायोः सिध्येत्केवलकुम्भकः ।
केवले कुम्भके सिद्धे रेचपूरविवर्जिते ।।५०।।

न तस्य दुर्लभं किंचित् त्रिषु लोकेषु विद्यते ।
प्रस्वेदो जायते पूर्वं मर्दनं तेन कारयेत ।।५१।।

ततो ऽपि धारणाद्वायोः क्रमेणैव शनैः ।
कम्पो भवति देहस्य आसनस्थस्य देहिनः ।।५२।।

ततो ऽधिकतराभ्यासाद्दार्दुरी स्वेद जायते ।
यथा च दर्दुरो भाव उत्प्लुत्योत्प्लुत्य गच्छति ।।५३।।

पद्मासनस्थितो योगी तथा गच्छति भूतले ।
ततो ऽधिकतराभ्यासाद्भूमित्यागश्च जायते ।।५४।।

पद्मासनस्थ एवासौ भूमिमुत्सृज्य वर्तते ।
अतिमानुषचेष्टादि तथा सामर्थ्यमुद्भवेत् ।।५५।।

न दर्शयेच्च सामर्थ्यं दर्शनं वीर्यवत्तरम् ।

स्वल्पं वा बहुधा दुःखं योगी न व्यथते तदा ।।५६।।

अल्पमूत्रपुरीषश्च स्वल्पनिद्रश्च जायते ।
कीलवो दूषिका लाला स्वेददुर्गन्धितानने ।।५७।।

एतानि सर्वथा तस्य न जायन्ते ततः परम् ।
ततो ऽधिकतराभ्यासाद्बलमुत्पद्यते बहु ।।५८।।

येन भूचर सिद्धिः स्याद्भूचराणां जये क्षमः ।
व्याघ्रो वा शरभो वापि गजो गवय एव वा ।।५९।।

सिंहो वा योगिना तेन मृचन्ते हस्तताडिताः ।
कन्दर्पस्य यथा रूपं तथा स्यादपि योगिनः ।।६०।।

तद्रूपवशगा नार्यः काङ्क्षन्ते तसय सङ्गमम् ।
यदि सङ्गं करोत्येष तस्य बिन्दुक्षयो भवेत् ।।६१।।

वर्जयित्वा स्त्रियाः सङ्गं कुर्यादभ्यासमादरात् ।
योगिनो ऽङ्गे सुगन्धश्च जायते बिन्दुधारणात् ।।६२।।

ततो रहस्युपाविष्टः प्रणवं प्लुतमात्रया ।
जपेत्पूर्वार्जितानां तु पापानां नाशहेतवे ।।६३।।

सर्वविघ्नहरो मन्त्रः प्रणवः सर्वदोषहा ।
एवमभ्यासयोगेन सिद्धिरारम्भसंभवा ।।६४।।

ततो भवेद्घटावस्था पवनाभ्यासतत्परा ।
प्राणो ऽपानो मनो बुद्धिर्जीवात्मपरमात्मनोः ।।६५।।

अन्योन्यस्याविरोधेन एकता घटते यदा ।
घटावस्थेति सा प्रोक्ता तच्चिह्नानि ब्रविम्यहम् ।।६६।।

पूर्वं यः कथितो ऽभ्यासश्चतुर्थांशं परिग्रहेत् ।
दिवा वा यदि वा सायं याममात्रं समभ्यसेत् ।।६७।।

एकवारं प्रतिदिनं कुर्यात्केवलकुम्भकम् ।
इन्द्रियाणीन्द्रियार्थेभ्यो यत्प्रत्याहरणं स्फुतम् ।।६८।।

योगी कुम्भकमास्थाय प्रत्याहार: स उच्यते ।
यद्यत्पश्यति चक्षुर्भ्यां तत्तदात्मेति भावयेत् ।।६९।।

यद्यच्छृणोति कर्णाभ्यां तत्तदात्मेति भावयेत् ।
लभते नासया यद्यत्तत्तदात्मेति भावयेत् ।।७०।।

जिह्वया यद्रसं ह्यत्ति तत्तदात्मेति भावयेत् ।
त्वचा यद्यत्स्पृशेद्योगी तत्तदात्मेति भावयेत् ।।७१।।

एवं ज्ञानेन्द्रियाणां तु तत्तत्सौख्यं सुसाधयेत् ।
याममात्रं प्रतिदिनं योगी यत्नादतन्द्रित: ।।७२।।

यथा वा चित्तसामर्थ्यं जायते योगिनो ध्रुवम् ।
दूरश्रुतिर्दूरदृष्टि: क्षणाद्दूरागमस्तथा ।।७३।।

वाक्सिद्धि: कामरूपत्वमदृश्यकरणी तथा ।
मलमूत्रप्रलेपेन लोहादेः स्वर्णता भवेत ।।७४।।

खे गतिस्तसय जायेत संतताभ्यासयोगत: ।
सदा बुद्धिमता भाव्यं योगिना योगसिद्धये ।।७५।।

एते विघ्ना महासिद्धेर्न रमेत्तेषु बुद्धिमान् ।
न दर्शयेत्स्वसामर्थ्यं यस्यकस्यापि योगिराट् ।।७६।।

यथा मूढो यथा मूर्खो यथा बधिर एव वा ।
तथा वर्तेत लोकस्य स्वसामर्थ्यस्य गुप्तये ।।७७।।

शिष्याश्च स्वस्वकार्येषु प्रार्थयन्ति न संशय: ।
तत्तत्कर्मकरव्यग्र: स्वाभ्यासे ऽविस्मृतो भवेत् ।।७८।।

अविस्मृत्य गुरोर्वाक्यमभ्यसेत्तदहर्निशम् ।
एवं भवेद्घठावस्था संतताभ्यासयोगतः ।।७९।।

अनभ्यासवतश्चैव वृथागोष्ठ्या न सिद्ध्यति ।
तस्मात्सर्वप्रयत्नेन योगमेव सदाभ्यसेत् ।।८०।।

ततः परिचयावस्था जायते ऽभ्यासयोगतः ।
वायुः परिचितो यत्नादग्निना सह कुण्डलीम् ।।८१।।

भावयित्वा सुषुम्नायां प्रविशेद्निरोधतः ।
वायुना सह चित्तं च प्रविशेच्च महापथम् ।।८२।।

यस्य चित्तं स्वपवनः सुषुम्नां प्रविशेदिह ।
भूमिरापो ऽनलो वायुराकाशश्चेति पञ्चकः ।।८३।।

येषु पञ्चसु देवानां धारणा पञ्चधोच्यते ।
पादादिजानुपर्यन्तं पृथिवीस्थानमुच्यते ।।८४।।

पृथिवी चतुरस्रं च पीतवर्णं लवर्णकम् ।
पार्थिवे वायुमारोप्य लकारेण समन्वितम् ।।८५।।

ध्यायंश्चतुर्भजाकारं चतुर्वक्त्रं हिरन्मयम् ।
धारयेत्पञ्च घटिकाः पृथिवीजयमाप्नुयात् ।।८६।।

पृथिवीयोगतो मृत्युर्न भवेदस्य योगिनः ।
आजानोः पायुपर्यन्तमापां स्थानं प्रकीर्तितम् ।।८७।।

आपो ऽर्धचन्द्रं शुक्लं च वंबीजं परिकीर्तितम् ।
वारुणे वायुमारोप्य वकारेण समन्वितम् ।।८८।।

स्मरन्नारायणं देवं चतुर्बाहुं किरीटिनम् ।
शुद्धस्फटिकसंकाशं पीतवाससमच्युतम् ।।८९।।

धारयेत्पञ्च घटिकाः सर्वपापैः प्रमुच्यते ।

ततो जलाद्भयं नास्ति जले मृत्युर्न विद्यते ।।९०।।

आपायोर्हृदयान्तं च वह्निस्थानं प्रकीर्तितम् ।
वह्निस्त्रिकोणं रक्तं च रेफाक्षरसमुद्भवम् ।।९१।।

वह्नौ चानिलमारोप्य रेफाक्षरसमुज्ज्वलम् ।
त्रियक्षं वरदं रुद्रं तरुणादित्यसंनिभम् ।।९२।।

भस्मोद्धूलितसर्वाङ्गं सुप्रसन्नमनुस्मरन् ।
धारयेत्पञ्च घटका वह्निनासौ न दह्यते ।।९३।।

न दह्यते शरीरं च प्रविष्टस्याग्निमण्डले ।
आहृदयाद्भ्रूवोर्मध्यं वायुस्थानं प्रकीर्तितम् ।।९४।।

वायुः षत्कोणकं कृष्णं यकाराक्षरभासुरम् ।
मारुतं मरुतां स्थाने यकाराक्षरभासुरम् ।।९५।।

धारयेत्तत्र सर्वज्ञमीश्वरं विश्वतोमुखम् ।
धारयेत्पञ्च घटिका वायुवद्योमगो भवेत् ।।९६।।

मरणं न तु वायोश्च भयं भवति योगिनः ।
आभ्रूमध्यात्तु मूर्धान्तमाकाशस्थानमुच्यते ।।९७।।

व्योम वृत्तं च धूम्रं च हकाराक्षरभासुरम् ।
आकशे वायुमारोप्य हकारोपरि शंकरम् ।।९८।।

बिन्दूरूपं महादेवं व्योमाकारं सदाशिवम् ।
शुद्धस्फटिकसंकाशं धृतबालेन्दुमौलिनम् ।।९९।।

पञ्चवक्त्रयुतं सौम्यं दशबाहुं त्रिलोचनम् ।
सर्वायुधैर्धृताकरं सर्वभूषणभूषितम् ।।१००।।

उमार्धदेहं वरदं सर्वकारणकारणम् ।
आकाशधारणात्तस्य खेचरत्वं भवेद्ध्रुवम् ।।१०१।।

यत्रकुत्र स्थितो वापि सुखमत्यन्तमश्नुते ।
एवं च धारणाः पञ्च कुर्याद्योगी विचक्षणः ।।१०२।।

ततो दृढशरीरः स्यान्मृत्युस्तस्य न विद्यते ।
ब्रह्मणः प्रलयेनापि न सीदति महामतिः ।।१०३।।

समभ्यसेत्तथा ध्यानं घटकाषष्टिमेव च ।
वायुं निरुध्य चाकाशे देवतामिष्टदामिति ।।१०४।।

सगणं ध्यानमेतत्स्यादणिमादिगुणप्रदम् ।
निर्गुणध्यानयुक्तस्य समाधिश्च ततो भवेत् ।।१०५।।

दिनद्वादशकेनैव समाधि समवाप्नुयात्
वायुं निरुध्य मेधावि जीवन्मुक्तो भवत्ययम् ।।१०६।।

समाधिः समतावस्था जीवात्मपरमात्मनोः ।
यदि स्वदेहमुत्स्रष्टुमिच्छा चेदुत्सृजेत्स्वयम् ।।१०७।।

परब्रह्मणि लीयेत न तस्योत्क्रान्तिरिष्यते ।
अथ नो चेत्समुत्स्रष्टुं स्वशरीरं प्रियं यदि ।।१०८।।

सर्वलोकेषु विहरन्नणिमादिगुणान्वितः ।
कदाचित्स्वेच्छया देवो भूत्वा स्वर्गे महीयते ।।१०९।।

मनुष्यो वापि यक्षो वा स्वेच्छयापीक्षणाद्भवेत् ।
सिंहो व्याघ्रो गजो वाश्वः स्वेच्छया हुतामियात् ।।११०।।

यथेष्टमेव वर्तेत यद्वा योगी महेश्वरः ।
अभ्यासभेदतो भेदः फलं तु सममेव हि ।।१११।।

पार्ष्णिं वामस्य पादस्य योनिस्थाने नियोजयेत् ।
प्रसार्य दक्षिणं पादं हस्ताभ्यां धारयेद्दृढम् ।।११२।।

चुबुकं हृदि विन्यस्य पूरयेद्वायुना पुनः ।
कुम्भकेन यथाशक्ति धारयित्वा तु रेचयेत् ।।११३।।

वामाङ्गेन समभ्यस्य दक्षाङ्गेन ततो ऽभ्यसेत् ।
प्रसारितस्तु यः पादस्तमूरूपरि नामयेत् ।।११४।।

अयमेव महाबन्ध उभयत्रैवमभ्यसेत् ।
महाबन्धस्थितो योगी कृत्वा पूरकमेकधीः ।।११५।।

वायुनां गतिमावृत्य निभृतं कण्ठमुद्रया ।
पुटद्वयं समाक्रम्य वायुः स्फुरति सत्वरम् ।।११६।।

अयमेव महावेधः सिद्धैरभ्यस्यते ऽनिशम् ।
अन्तःकपालकुहरे जिह्वां व्यावृत्य धारयेत् ।।११७।।

भ्रूमध्यदृष्टिरप्येषा मुद्रा भवति खेचरी ।
कण्ठमाकुञ्चय हृदये स्थापयेद्दृढया धिया ।।११८।।

बन्धो जालंधराख्यो ऽयं मृत्युमातङ्ककेसरी ।
बन्धो येन सुषुम्नायां प्राणस्तूड्डीयते यतः ।।११९।।

उड्डयानाख्यो हि बन्धो ऽयं योगिभिः समुदाहृतः ।
पार्ष्णिभागेन सम्पीड्य योनिमाकुञ्चयेद्दृढम् ।।१२०।।

अपानमूर्ध्वमुत्थाप्य योनिबन्धो ऽयमुच्यते ।
प्राणापानौ नादबिन्दू मूलबन्धेन चैकताम् ।।१२१।।

गत्वा योगस्य संसिद्धिं यच्छतो नात्र संशयः ।
करणी विपरीताख्या सर्वव्याधिविनाशिनी ।।१२२।।

नित्यमभ्यासयुक्तस्य जाठराग्निविवर्धनी ।
आहारो बहुलस्तस्य संपाद्यः साधकस्य च ।।१२३।।

अल्पाहारो यदि भवेदग्निर्देहं हरेत्क्षणात् ।
अधःशिरश्चोर्ध्वपादः क्षणं स्यात्प्रथमे दिने ।।१२४।।

क्षणात्तु किंचिदधिकमभ्यसेत्तु दिनेदिने ।
वली च पलितं चैव सण्मासार्धान्न दृश्यते ।।१२५।।

याममात्रं तु यो नित्यमभ्यसेत्स तु कालजित् ।
वज्रोलीमभ्यसेद्यस्तु स योगी सिद्धिभाजनम् ।।१२६।।

लभ्यते यदि तस्यैव योगसिद्धिः करे स्थिता ।
अतीतानागतं वेत्ति खेचरी च भवेद्ध्रुवम् ।।१२७।।

अमरीं यः पिबेन्नित्यं नस्यं कुर्वन्दिने ।
वज्रोलीमभ्यसेन्नित्यममरोलीति कथ्यते ।।१२८।।

ततो भवेद्राजयोगो नान्तरा भवति ध्रुवम् ।
यदा तु राजयोगेन निष्पन्ना योगिभिः क्रिया ।।१२९।।

तदा विवेकवैराग्यं जायते योगिनो ध्रुवम् ।
विष्णुर्नाम महायोगी महाभूतो महातपाः ।।१३०।।

तत्त्वमार्गे तथा दीपो दृश्यते पुरुषोत्तमः ।
यः स्तनः पूर्वपीतस्तं निष्पीड्य मुदमश्नुते ।।१३१।।

यस्माज्जातो भगात्पूर्वं तस्मिन्नेव भगे रमन् ।
या माता सा पुनर्भार्या या भार्या मातरेव हि ।।१३२।।

यः पिता स पुनः पुत्रो यः पुत्रः स पुनः पिता ।
एवं संसारचक्रेण कूपचक्रे घटा इव ।।१३३।।

भ्रमन्तो योनिजन्मानि श्रुत्वा लोकान्समश्नुते ।
त्रयो लोकास्त्रयो वेदास्तिस्रः संध्यास्त्रयः स्वराः ।।१३४।।

त्रयो ऽग्नयश्च त्रिगुणाः स्थिताः सर्वे त्रयाक्षरे ।
त्रयाणामक्षराणां च यो ऽधीते ऽप्यर्धमक्षरम् ।।१३५।।

तेन सर्वमिदं प्रोतं तत्सत्यं तत्परं पदम् ।
पुष्पमध्ये यथा गन्धः पयोमध्ये यथा घृतम् ।।१३६।।

तिलमध्ये यथा तैलं पाषाणेष्विव काञ्चनम् ।
हृदि स्थाने स्थितं पद्मं तस्य वक्त्रमधोमुखम् ।।१३७।।

ऊर्ध्वनालमधोबिन्दुस्तस्य मध्ये स्थितं मनः ।
अकारे रेचितं पद्ममुकारेणैव भिद्यते ।।१३८।।

मकारे लभते नादमर्धमात्रा तु निश्चला ।
शुद्धस्फटिकसंकाशं निष्कलं पापनाशनम् ।।१३९।।

लभते योगयुक्तात्मा पुरुषसस्तत्परं पदम् ।
कूर्मः स्वपाणिपादादिशिरश्चात्मनि धारयेत् ।।१४०।।

एवं द्वारेषु सर्वेषु वायुपूरितरेचितः ।
निषिद्धे तु नवद्वारे ऊर्ध्वं प्राश्वसंस्तथा ।।१४१।।

घटमध्ये यथा दीपो निवातं कुम्भकं विदुः ।
निषिद्धैर्नवभिर्वीरैर्निर्जने निरुपद्रवे ।।१४२।।

निश्चितं त्वात्ममात्रेणावशिष्टं योगसेवया ।।
इत्युपनिषत् ।।

2. Transcription Pronunciation Guide

a	nut	ṭ	borscht
ā	father	ṭh	borscht home
i	bit	ḍ	fresh dill
ī	knee	ḍh	flushed heart
u	hook	ṇ	rainy
ū	sue	t	tarp
ṛ	hurt	th	scout hall
e	net	d	modern
ai	time	dh	mud hut
o	got	n	banal
au	house	p	papa
ṃ	hum	ph	top half
ḥ	h + preceding vowel	b	maybe
k	paprika	bh	mob hall
kh	ink horn	m	chroma
g	ago	y	young
gh	big hut	r	merit
ṅ	anger	l	alas
c	chat	v	lava
ch	much harm	ś	shin
j	jog	ṣ	sunshine
jh	raj house	h	hut
ñ	engine		

3. Translation

Invocation
The blessed one is born in the divine auspiciousness of yoga and emancipation. I worship the feet of Rāma, who is the essence of yoga, arisen from Viṣṇu. Saying: Om, may this teaching benefit both of us together. Peace.

1.
I shall describe the essence of Yoga, with the desire of benefiting the yogis. He, who has both heard and studied this, is freed from all evils.

2.
The great yogin, the great being, the great ascetic is Viṣṇu by name. He, the Supreme Spirit, is seen like a light on the way to the essence.

3.
The paternal grandfather (Brahma), having served and prostrated to the protector of the world (Viṣṇu), asked him: 'Describe to me the essence of yoga and the joining together of its eight components'.

4.
Hṛṣīkeśa said to him: 'Listen, I will explain thoroughly: living beings are always trapped by the web of illusion in happiness and sorrow.

5, 6.
But, *kaivalya*, the supreme abode, is difficult to reach by different ways. Of these, the way (to kaivalya) is the one which leads to liberation, destroying the web of illusion, eliminating birth, death, old age [and] disease, [and] delivering [the aspirant] from death. Those fallen among the web of teachings are deluded by that knowledge.

7.
[It is] not possible even for the gods to describe a place [which is] indescribable. How can a form [already] illuminated by its own self be illuminated by [any] teachings?

8.
Just that, [which is] undivided, unsullied, calm and has gone beyond all welfare, is chosen by a living form with the fruits of good and evil deeds.

9.
How did that, which is the seat of the supreme soul, eternal [and] beyond the state of all existing things, [and is] pure [and] has the form of wisdom, pass to [the state] of the living?

10.
There, the *ahaṃkāra* brought forth in this, like [a bubble] suddenly arising in the water, a body consisting of the five elements, of the three *guṇas*, and bound by the seven *dhātus*.

11.
Perceive that which is joined with happiness and sorrow, which has been purified, is through the production of *jīva.* Thus the term *jīva* is revealed in the supreme self.

12, 13.
That embodied soul is thought [to be] complete [when] freed from these faults: desire, anger, fear and also delusion, greed, pride, lust, birth and death, miserliness, grief, laziness, hunger, thirst, craving, shame, fear, sorrow, despair and exultation as well.

14.
Thus I shall tell you the means and purpose for the destruction of these faults. How can that knowledge, which omits yoga, be sure to give liberation?

15.
But surely yoga without *jñāna* [is] not favourable for the effect of liberation. Thus the seeker of liberation must be established in both jñāna and yoga.

16.
The cycle of samsara (birth, death and rebirth) [occurs] only due to *ajñāna* (ignorance) [and] is released through jñāna (knowledge). In the beginning, jñāna [was] indeed the very embodiment of knowledge [and was] the only means for jñāna to be understood.

17.
By it (jñāna), the supreme seat is known directly as the indwelling, pure, undivided form of *kaivalya*, consisting of the form of s*at-cit-ānanda*.

18.
[It is] beyond the knowledge and appearance [of] creation, maintenance and dissolution. Thus, this was said about jñāna. Now I shall describe yoga to you.

19.
O Brahman, yoga is divided into many parts, namely: mantra yoga, laya yoga and haṭha yoga, as well; that is in accordance with rāja yoga.

20.
Therefore, the beginning stage, the second, third and indeed the fourth and final stage [are] prescribed, and thus [this] state is always proclaimed.

21, 22.
O Brahman, listen! I shall describe concisely the characteristic[s] of these [yogas]. Whoever should repeat the mantra for twelve years together with the syllables, gradually obtains jñāna, beginning with the power of making the body subtle and light, and the knowledge of guṇa, the qualities of nature. The most inferior aspirant of low intelligence practises this yoga.

23.
Laya Yoga, dissolution of individual consciousness, is described in innumerable ways. One should meditate on the absolute Lord [while] moving, resting, sleeping [or] eating.

24, 25.
This must be laya yoga. Listen to that which is haṭha yoga. Yoga is said [to have] eight limbs: yama and niyama, and indeed āsana, prāṇāyāma, pratyāhāra, dhāraṇā, and dhyāna (meditation on Vishnu at the eyebrow centre), [leading to] samādhi, the state of equilibrium.

26, 27.
[This yoga also includes practices of mudrā and bandha:] mahā mudrā, mahā bandha and mahā vedha, khecarī mudrā, jālandhara bandha, uḍḍiyāna bandha, and likewise mūla bandha, [as well as] chanting the mantra Aum for a long time, listening to the highest truth, and the triad of vajrolī, amarolī and sahajolī.

28, 29.
O Brahman, listen attentively to each characteristic of these [limbs]. Amongst the yamas, light eating is the single chief factor. Amongst the niyamas, non-violence is definitely the most important, O four-faced one. Likewise, [there are] four [main postures]: siddhāsana, padmāsana, siṃhāsana and bhadrāsana.

30, 31.

But, O Four-faced One, the following obstacles [arise]: time of early practice, laziness, boasting, the company of fraudulent people, beginning sadhana with mantra, desire for metals and women etc, [and] indeed illusions of craving and greed. Knowing [this], a wise man should relinquish all obstacles through [his] virtuous powers.

32, 33.

Now he should make a beautiful monastic hut with a narrow doorway, without cracks, well-smeared with cow-dung or mortar, and carefully cleared of bugs, mosquitoes [and] spiders. Then, having gone into padmāsana, he should practise prāṇāyāma by himself.

34.

Every day [the sādhana kutir should be] specially swept with a broom, imbued with pleasant fragrances and perfumed with sweet-smelling gum.

35, 36a.

Having sat down there [and] assumed padmāsana on a cushion of cloth, deerskin [and] kuśa grass, not very high [and] not very low, the wise man, his body upright and his clasped hands respectfully outstretched, should bow down to his personal deity.

36b, 37, 38.

Then, having closed his right nostril with the thumb of his right hand, he should inhale very slowly through the left nostril, and then, without pausing, he should perform breath retention for as long as he can. He should exhale again through the right nostril quite slowly, not quickly. Having inhaled through the right nostril again, he should slowly fill the inner area.

39.
Having retained [the breath for] as long as possible, he should exhale slowly through the left nostril. Through whichever nostril he exhales, inhaling [again] through it, he should retain [the breath] without interruption.

40.
This is declared: the mātrā, unit of time, [is measured] by making [a circle] to the right [with the hand] on the knee, neither quickly nor slowly, [and then] he should snap his thumb.

41, 42.
Having directed the inhaled breath slowly through the left nostril for sixteen mātrās, he should then retain [the breath] fully for sixty four mātrās. He should exhale again through the right nostril for thirty two mātrās. Having inhaled again through the right nostril as before [he should become] established [in the practice].

43.
He should practise four times a day: in the morning, at midday, in the evening and at midnight, slowly [increasing] up to eighty breath retentions.

44, 45.
After practising in this way for three months, there should then be purification of the nāḍīs. When there is purification of the nāḍīs, then external signs are produced in the body of the yogin. I shall describe them fully: lightness of the body, radiance, increase of digestive fire.

46.
And then it should surely bring about leanness of the body. One who is accomplished in yoga should avoid foods [which] obstruct [the practice of] yoga.

47, 48, 49.
He should give up salt, mustard and [food which is] sour and hot, dry and pungent, vegetables of every kind, asafoetida etc, enjoyment of [the warmth of] fire, women and travel, bathing in the morning, fasting etc, and [whatever gives] distress to the body. During the period of yoga practice, food of milk and ghee is ordained the best. Wheat, horse beans and boiled rice are known for their development of yoga. Then he should be most capable of suspension of the breath for as long as he wishes.

50, 51a
Kevala kumbhaka, spontaneous breath retention, is attained by holding the breath inside for as long as possible. When perfected in spontaneous breath retention, exhaling [and] inhaling are given up. There exists nothing unattainable by him in the three worlds.

51b, 52, 53a.
At first perspiration is produced; therefore it should be cleaned. Then again, in the course of slowly holding the breath, the person experiences tremor in the body, while sitting. Then, from much more practice, frog-like sweat is produced.

53b, 54, 55.
And, just as the frog moves up by leaps and bounds, thus the yogin moves [while] seated in padmāsana on the ground. Then, because of much more practice, rising up [from] the earth is accomplished, and that person, having levitated from the earth, still remains seated in padmāsana. Thus the power for superhuman action and other things may arise.

56.
He should not reveal [this] teaching [whose] power [is] heroically inspired. Then the yogin is not affected by hardship, [whether] very small or great.

57, 58a.
Little urine and excrement are produced, and [there is] very little sleep. [When] indeed, rheum of the eyes, saliva, sweat and bad smell are negligible, then subsequently these things do not arise in him at all.

58b, 59, 60a.
Then, after a lot more practice, great strength arises, by which he attains bhūcara siddhi, which gives him the power to move through mountains and walls, and mastery over all creatures moving on the earth. Thus the deer, lion, tiger, or even elephant or wild bull perish, when struck by the hand of this yogin.

60b, 61.
The *yogin* is just like the form of *Kāma*, the god of love. Women enthralled by such an appearance desire intercourse with him. If he makes [this] connection, then there will be a decrease of his semen.

62.
Having given up intercourse with woman, he should do [his] practice seriously. By preserving the semen, a pleasant fragrance is produced in the body of the yogin.

63.
Then, seated in a secret [place], he should repeat *Aum* with prolonged mātrās for the purpose of the destruction of previously committed sins.

64.
The mantra *Aum* destroys all obstacles [and] removes all faults. In this way, by the practice of yoga, he enters into the first *siddhi*.

65, 66.
Then, following upon that, with practice on the breath, is the second state. When union takes place with each other without conflict, between *prāṇa* and *apāna*, *manas* and *buddhi*, *jīvātmā* and *paramātmā*, this is declared the second state. I shall describe its signs.

67, 68a.
He should undertake one fourth of the practice described before. He should practise only one restraint, either by day or at night. He should do *kevala kumbhaka* once every day.

68b, 69, 70, 71, 72.
Complete withdrawal of the sense organs from the objects of the senses by strenuous retention of the breath is called *pratyāhāra*. Whatever the yogin then sees with his eyes, this is to be declared ātman. Whatever he then hears with his ears, this is to be declared ātman. Whatever he then smells through his nose, this is to be declared ātman. Whatever he then tastes with his tongue, this is to be declared ātman. Whatever he then touches with his skin, this is to be declared ātman. Thus, with undaunted effort, for the welfare of the sensory organs, the yogin should control them for a period of two hours every day.

73, 74, 75.
Just as the *yogin*'s power of mind becomes stable, then arises clairaudience, clairvoyance, [the ability to] travel far within a moment, [great] power of speech, the ability to assume any form desired, [and] to become invisible, [and to turn] iron, [when] smeared with excrement and urine, into gold. The wise *yogin* must always be assiduously [and] continuously practising for attainment in yoga. [Then] levitation should be possible for him.

76, 77, 78a.
These great powers [are] obstacles. The wise man should not delight in them. The king of yogins should not display his own ability to anyone, whosoever. He should live in the world like a fool, an idiot or even a deaf person, thus guarding his own power. There is no doubt his disciples would beg [him to reveal his powers] for their own purposes.

78b, 79.
However, he who is occupied with working for others should not forget his own practice. Not forgetting the words of the guru, then he should practise day and night. Thus, assiduously and continuously practising, he becomes (enters) the second state.

80, 81a.
And indeed, he does not gain by useless company [which leads to] neglect of practice. Therefore he should always practise yoga with complete devotion. Then, through strenuous practice, the third state (of yoga) is attained.

81b, 82, 83a.
The breath, after much effort, having stimulated the
kuṇḍalinī with fire, knowingly enters the suṣumnā without interruption. When one's own vital energy enters the citta with the breath, it ascends hither the great path of the suṣumnā.

83b, 84a.
It is said there are five [elements]: earth, water, fire, air and ether. In these five the attention of the deities is said [to be] five-fold.

84b, 85, 86, 87a.
It is said that the site of *pṛthvī*, the earth element, begins at the feet and ends at the knees. (The symbol for) pṛthvī is a yellow square, and the bīja mantra, or seed sound, is *lam*.

Directing the breath within the area of the earth element together with the sound *lam*, meditating on and performing worship to the four faced, golden one, he should concentrate for two hours. [Thus] he would obtain victory over the earth. Death is not for this yogin, who has united with the earth element.

87b, 88, 89, 90.
The area from the knees up to the anus is named āpas, water element. [The symbol is] a white half-moon and its bīja mantra is vam. Directing the breath within the region of the water element together with the sound vam, remembering the four-armed, imperishable god Nārāyana, adorned with a crown, with the appearance of pure crystal, [and wearing] an orange garment, he should concentrate for two hours, [and then] he is freed from all sins. Thus there is no fear of water, [as his] death does not occur in water.

91, 92, 93, 94a.
From (the region of) water to the heart is called the site of *agni*, the fire element. (The symbol of) agni is a red triangle, and it is the source of the subtle sound *ram*. He should concentrate for two hours, directing the vital air, radiant with the mantra *ram,* within the fire element. Remembering Rudra, this dazzling sovereign, the three-eyed one, who grants boons, who resembles the newly risen sun, whose limbs are all smeared with ash, that one is not burned by fire. The body is not burned, even when it has entered the fire-pit.

94b, 95, 96, 97a.
From the heart to the eyebrow centre is called the site of *vāyu*, the air element. [The symbol of] vāyu is hexagonal in shape, blue in color, and glows with the vibration of *yam*. He should concentrate for two hours on the vital air, radiating the vibration *yam,* at the site of vāyu, and then on the all-knowing Īśwara, the Supreme Being, who has faces on all

sides. The siddhi of levitation arises through mastery of vāyu. Fear of wind [is overcome, because wind] cannot cause the death of the yogin.

97b, 98, 99, 100, 101, 102a.

Now, it is said, the site of *ākāśa* is from the eyebrow centre to the crown of the head. The (symbol of the) ether element is a smokey-grey circle, and it glows with the vibration *ham*. Directing the breath upwards within (the region of) ākāśa [he should] repeat the sound *ham.* (The deity of ākāśa is) Sadāśiva, who is tranquil, with the form of bindu, and the shape of vyoma. (He) shines like pure crystal, and is wearing a crescent moon on his head. (He) has five faces with pleasing expressions [and] three eyes. His ten arms hold all weapons [and are] adorned with all ornaments. Uma resides within half of his body, granting boons. That yogin who concentrates within ākāśa on the supreme deity, Sadāśiva, who is the cause of all causes, will certainly be able to levitate, and also enjoy endless happiness wherever he is.

102b, 103.

And so the accomplished yogin should perform [these] five dhāraṇās. Then his body becomes strong [and] death is not known to him. The wise man does not perish, even at the time of *pralaya*, when the universe is dissolved back into Brahma.

104, 105, 106.

Then, holding the breath in the ether element, he should practise deep meditation on the deity with form and qualities, who grants his wishes, for six *ghaṭikas* (two hours and twenty four minutes). It is said this is *saguṇa dhyāna*, meditation on form, which bestows attributes, beginning with anima, the power of making the body small and subtle. And thus he is merged in *nirguṇa dhyāna*, formless meditation, and attains *samādhi,* transcendental meditation. He should obtain this within just twelve days. Having retained the breath, this wise one becomes a *jīvanmukta,* liberated while still living in the body.

107, 108.
Samādhi is the state [in which] the individual soul and the cosmic soul [are] the same. If (the yogin) desires to abandon the body, this can be accomplished by himself. Being attached to the supreme reality, he does not seek to ascend.

109, 110, 111.
Endowed with attributes, such as *aṇimā,* the power of making the body minute and subtle, he moves within all the worlds. At times, having become a *deva,* divine being, through his own will, he is highly honoured in the celestial world. Or, through his own will, he may even take the appearance of a man or a *yakṣa,* demi-god. By his own will, he may move in many forms, [such as] a lion, tiger, elephant or horse. The *yogin,* who is like the supreme lord, exists in accordance with his own wishes. [There is] a difference in the various practices, but indeed the result is the same.

112, 113, 114, 115a.
He should press the heel of the left foot in the region of the perineum. Having extended the right leg, he should hold [it] firmly with both hands. Placing the chin on the chest, he should inhale again. Maintaining breath retention for as long as possible, he should then exhale. Having practised with the left foot, he should then practise with the right. He should then bend whichever leg is stretched out against the thigh. This is *mahābandha*; in this way it should be practised on both sides.

115b, 116, 117a.
The *yogin*, (sitting) in the position of mahābandha, having inhaled, with his mind still, stops the flow of the prāṇas by means of the throat lock. The two nāḍīs, iḍā and piṅgalā,

having entered (suṣumnā), the prāṇa vibrates quickly. This is *mahāvedha*; it is practised continually by the siddhas.

117b, 118a.
Folding the tongue back within the cavity inside the head, he should fix the gaze on the point between the eyebrows; then this is khecarī mudrā.

118b, 119a.
Contracting the throat, he should place [the chin] on the chest with focused mind. This is called jālandhara bandha [and] is a lion to the fear of death.

119b, 120a.
Now that bandha by which the prāṇa flies upward through suṣumnā is called uḍḍiyāna bandha by the yogins.

120b, 121a.
He should firmly contract the perineum by means of pressure with part of the heel, raising the *apāna* upwards; this is called *yoni bandha.*

121b, 122, 123, 124a.
Prāṇa/apāna and *nāda/bindu*, are united through (the practice of) moolabandha (combined with) viparīta karaṇī (mudrā). Success in yoga is attained by one who engages in this practice regularly; there is no doubt here. This practice is said to increase the digestive fire, removing all diseases. An abundance of food should be brought and consumed by the aspirant. If little is supplied, the fire will immediately take his body.

124b, 125, 126a.
On the first day [his] head should be on the ground and [his] legs raised up for a moment. Every day he should practise a little longer. Wrinkles and even grey hair will not be seen

after six and a half months. Indeed, whoever practises continuously for a period of three hours conquers time.

126b, 127.
Indeed whoever practises vajrolī is a yogin [and] the recipient of siddhis. If accomplishment in yoga is ever attained by him, it is lasting. He knows the events of the past and certainly has the power of flight.

128, 129a.
Whoever always drinks the mid-stream of urine daily, taking [it] through the nose, [and] always practises vajrolī, is said [to be a practitioner of] amarolī. Then he attains rāja yoga, [and] there is certainly no distance [between him and enlightenment].

129b, 130, 131a.
When kriyā is brought about by yogins through rāja yoga, then the yogins are certainly victorious in *viveka* and *vairagya.* The supreme spirit, Viṣṇu, who is the great yogin, lord of the elements and master of austerities, is then seen as a light on the path of the true reality.

131b, 132, 133, 134a.
That breast from which he drank before, he obtains joy by fondling, [and] he delights in that very organ from which he was previously born. She who was his wife is now his mother, and she who is now his mother will again be his wife. He who is the father will again be the son, and he who is the son will again be the father. Hearing [this], he abides in the worlds, in the same way as the beings wandering through the wheel of *saṃsāra*, like a jar in a water-wheel.

134b, 135, 136a.
The three worlds, three Vedas, three *sandhyās*, three *swaras*, three fires and the three *guṇas* are all placed in the three imperishable sounds [of *Aum*], and whoever has delved into

even half a sound is pervaded by all this. This [is] the Truth; this [is] the Supreme Seat.

136b, 137, 138, 139a.
As the fragrance within the flower, as the ghee within the milk, as the oil within the sesame, as the gold within the rock, [so] is the lotus placed in the area of the heart. Its face is bent down; its stalk is upright. Its *bindu* is below; within it abides *manas*. The lotus is expanded with the sound A; with the sound U, it is opened up; by the sound M, it obtains sound, and the half syllable is still.

139b, 140a.
The person whose self is united with yoga obtains that supreme seat, [which] has the appearance of pure crystal, [is] undivided [and] destroys sins.

140b, 141, 142.
The tortoise holds within itself its own hands, feet and also head, so is the air inhaled and exhaled in all the orifices [of the body]. Then, drawing in the breath forwards and upwards, when the nine orifices are restrained, like a lamp inside a jar, the stillness of kumbhaka is known by adepts, who have restrained the nine orifices in a deserted place, free from disturbances.

Conclusion
Through dedication to yoga, you surely [will realise] that the ātmās, the highest consciousness, alone remains. Thus ends the Upaniṣad.

ABOUT THE AUTHOR

Swami Satyadharma is a senior sannyasin and versatile teacher of yogic meditation and allied philosophies, having a Master of Arts in Yoga Philosophy with First Class Honors from Bihar Yoga Bharati, India. She wrote the commentary on the *Yoga Chudamani Upanishad*, which was published by Yoga Publications Trust in 2003. Born in Connecticut USA, she lived in India for over 35 years under the direct tutelage of her yoga master, Swami Satyananda Saraswati, where she imbibed the traditional yogic teachings, and became Director of the Department of Undergraduate Studies at Bihar Yoga Bharati. She has compiled and edited many major yoga publications, such as *Yoga Darshan, Sannyasa Darshan, Dharana Darshan* and the *Teachings of Swami Satyananda.* After travelling for many years throughout Europe, USA, Asia and Australia, giving lectures and seminars, she now lives a life of sadhana and introspection in Australia, while continuing to elucidate the ancient teachings of yoga in the form of the twenty Yoga Upanishads.

ABOUT THE TRANSLATOR

Srimukti (Ruth Perini) was for many years a teacher of yoga and meditation. Already a linguist, having graduated in French, Italian and Japanese from the Universities of Sydney and Queensland, Australia, she undertook four years of studies in Sanskrit at the Australian National University (ANU) with Dr McComas Taylor. She was invited to join the Golden Key International Society for outstanding academic achievement, as she was awarded High Distinctions throughout her Sanskrit studies. She has also translated the *Yoga Darśana* and *Nāda Bindu, Dhyānabindu, Yoga Kuṇḍalī Upaniṣads*, and is currently working on the *Varāha Upaniṣad.*

Ruth (Srimukti) may be contacted on yoga.upanishads@yahoo.com.

www.ingramcontent.com/pod-product-compliance
Lightning Source LLC
Chambersburg PA
CBHW070252010526
44107CB00056B/2436
* 9 7 8 0 6 4 8 9 1 0 7 1 8 *